THE GROUP LEADER'S TOOLKIT

ENERGISING

MOTIVATION

PROBLEM SOLVING

ASSESSING & EVALUATING

CLOSURES

MANAGING BEHAVIOUR

ICE BREAKERS

BUILDING TRUST

Activities & Strategies for Working with Groups

Robin Dynes

Speechmark

For the sake of clarity alone, the masculine pronoun 'he' is used in the activity descriptions to refer to the group participant.

First published in 2006 by

Speechmark Publishing Ltd, 8 Oxford Court, St James Road, Brackley NN13 7XY, UK

Tel: +44 (0) 1280 845 570 Fax: +44 (0) 1280 845 584

www.speechmark.net

002-5312/Printed in the United Kingdom/1010

British Library Cataloguing in Publication Data

Dynes Robin

   The group leader's toolkit : activities and strategies for working with groups

   1. Social group work 2. Group relations training

   I. Title

   361.4

ISBN-13: 978 0 86388 565 5

ISBN-10: 0 86388 565 9

Contents

List of resources

The resources and materials used in the activities are readily available in most day centres, hospitals, education centres and venues where the activities are likely to take place. Many of the activities require no materials. This makes them easy to use in all settings. Below is a complete list.

Sticky labels

Adhesive notes

Safety pins

Blank cards

Red, amber and green cards

Material to be used as blindfolds

Envelopes

Crayons

A poster

Plant bulbs

A ruler or biscuit tin

Flipchart/chalkboard/whiteboard

Magic markers

Chalk

Paper

Pens

Pencils

Soft balls

Cushions

A hat or cap

Chocolate or sweets for prizes

Cardboard boxes or masking tape

DVD recorder

Video camera and player

Tape recorder and player

CDs and player

Recorded music

A variety of magazines

Drawing pins/Blu-Tack

The Group Leader's Toolkit

Activities listed by theme

8 Assessment and evaluation

9 Additional tools

10 Closures

Preface

The Group Leader's Toolkit has developed over the years to meet the requirements of the many groups in which I have been involved. The activities have been adapted from many different sources, mostly friends and colleagues who are also involved in facilitating groups. When I have discovered a new activity it has been hastily noted, adapted and used in groups that I have facilitated in many different environments. These include staff training courses, youth centres, probation units, day centres, psychiatric hospitals and education centres.

No toolkit can be fully comprehensive. However, most of the activities in this book can be adapted in a wide variety of ways. Use these activities as a starting point for your own work; adapt, change and fill in the gaps to suit your own working environment and needs.

Robin Dynes

Acknowledgements

I would like to thank the many colleagues I have worked with over the years who have so generously shared many of the activities and adaptations of games in this book. They include social workers, occupational therapists, nursing staff, psychologists, drama therapists, tutors, psychiatrists and counsellors. In particular I thank Marylyn, Adele, Barbara, Liz, Dave, Jeannette, June, Joan, Bob, Lesley, Lyn, Anna, Angie and Caroline. What a joy it has been to work with you all. Most of all, I would like to salute the many clients and students from whom I have learned so much and who have enriched my life. Thank you.

Introduction
The idea behind this book

The Group Leader's Toolkit provides a collection of easily prepared activities, games and strategies to supplement the main content of group sessions. They can be used in most types of group, including:

- → skills training groups
- → educational groups
- → youth groups
- → developmental groups
- → psycho-educational groups

- → counselling groups
- → therapy groups
- → personal growth groups
- → mutual support groups
- → problem solving groups

When preparing a group session, you will probably start by planning the main areas you want to cover. For example, in an assertiveness training session the principal activities might have the heading titles, 'What does being assertive mean?', 'Identifying different types of behaviour', 'Owning your own feelings', and so on. Once you have prepared the most important items of the session you then need extra ingredients to ensure it runs smoothly and as an integrated whole. This is where the Group Leader's Toolkit is a useful supplement, providing ideas for activities in the following areas:

- → introducing people to each other
- → setting goals
- → building trust
- → encouraging people to work together
- → energising the group
- → changing the group mood
- → raising self-awareness
- → providing a quick assessment
- → obtaining feedback
- → reflection and learning from experience

- → motivating people
- → encouraging personal responsibility
- → stimulating learning
- → aiding creative thinking
- → overcoming obstacles
- → linking sessions
- → helping with problem solving
- → identifying change
- → evaluating the group, individuals or facilitators
- → ending the group

Who is the toolkit for?

The Group Leader's Toolkit provides a range of indispensable tools for anyone who works with groups. This includes teachers, occupational therapists, nurses, social workers, psychologists, youth workers, probation officers, support workers or anyone facilitating groups in day centres, residential homes, education centres, hospitals, youth centres and schools.

Using the toolkit

The toolkit contains 150 ideas for working with groups. Variations on the core acitivity show how the games may be adapted to suit particular groups. These are divided into sections to make it easy to find the tool you want for a particular group. The sections are:

1   Introductions and icebreakers
2   Building trust
3   Energising
4   Stimulating learning
5   Motivation
6   Problem solving
7   Managing behaviour and personal responsibility
8   Assessment and evaluation
9   Additional tools
10 Closures

Each activity is presented in an easy-to-use format:

AIMS

The main aims of the activities are given. However, the list is not exhaustive and the activities can be adapted and used for other purposes (see 'Use also for ...', below). Feel free to use them as described. Whatever the reason for using an activity, ensure that the objectives are made clear when introducing it to a group and that the participants understand why they are doing it.

PREPARATION *materials needed*

Many activities require little or no preparation and on the whole, all you have to do is flip through the book and decide which idea you want to use. A list of materials needed for an activity is given where necessary. Making an effort to gather together the materials is worthwhile, as most will lend themselves to repeated use. It would be useful to have available a stock of paper, pens, pencils, magic markers, a flipchart, chalkboard or whiteboard. A comprehensive list of resources is given on page v.

THE ACTIVITY

The activities are designed to be used flexibly. Do adapt the procedure to meet the needs of particular groups. Treat each activity as adaptable and amend or add to it as you see fit.

VARIATION

This section shows how the activity and procedure can be adapted to meet group needs.

COMMENT

Useful tips and suggestions about using the activities are given.

USE ALSO FOR

The activities are adaptable and lend themselves to use under several different section headings. Some of these secondary purposes are listed at the foot of the activity, under this heading.

Integrating the activities

Try to link the activities with what is to follow or has gone before, both in topic and in mood. This can be accomplished by making statements such as, 'I didn't think the last exercise went very well; this time can we …?' Even if you want to use an activity to provide a rest and it has no connection with the other parts of the session, you should still make your reasons clear: for example, 'Everyone has been working very hard, I feel we all need a bit of a rest and some fun. Let's …' If you need feedback on how much has been learned you might say something like, 'I have given you a lot of information. I would like to check your understanding of it before moving on.'

A list of activities, arranged by theme, is provided on pages vi–viii.

Introductions and icebreakers

Activities to help participants get to know each other, to make it easier for them to be in a group, to encourage participation and to break down barriers.

Famous people

AIMS
↑ To help participants get to know each other
↑ To identify influences on beliefs
↑ To enable people to feel at ease and start making disclosures
↑ To have fun

PREPARATION *materials needed*

None.

THE ACTIVITY

Ask the group members to think of a famous person whom they admire. What qualities does that person have that they respect? Allow a pause for thought, then ask each group member, in turn, to state his own name, the famous person he admires and the qualities he respects in this person.

VARIATION

Instead of using famous people, have group members think about a personal acquaintance who has influenced them in some way. They state who the person was and in what way they have been influenced.

COMMENT

This is a non-threatening method of introducing group members to each other and enabling them to start making disclosures. If you like, you can alternate between a round using famous people and a round using personal acquaintances.

USE ALSO FOR

Building trust, energising and motivation.

Word association

PREPARATION *materials needed*

Have available a short list of words to stimulate associated memories. Examples are: spring, school, food, journey, holiday, Christmas, animals, and so on. Write the words up on a flipchart, chalkboard or whiteboard.

AIMS

↑ To help group members get to know each other better
↑ To begin building trust
↑ To encourage self-disclosure

THE ACTIVITY

Ask the group members to choose a word that stimulates a memory for them. It might be something that happened at Christmas, a special or difficult journey they made, or an animal they became attached to. After a pause for thought, participants, in turn, state their name and the word chosen – and share the memory. If a wide choice of words is used, a second round of memories can be completed if required.

VARIATION

Instead of using words as stimulae, cut some pictures of places from magazines, for example mountains, beaches, sports scenes, and so on. Display the pictures and invite participants to choose a picture that stimulates a memory. Each participant then states his name, shows the picture and recounts the associated memory.

COMMENT

Group members will be encouraged to participate if you start by sharing one association of your own with a word or picture. Words used for association can be chosen to suit particular groups. The activity provides a light-hearted method of preparing group members to make personal disclosures in all types of settings.

USE ALSO FOR

Building trust, energising and motivation.

 **Personal possessions**

AIMS

↑ To introduce group members to each other

↑ To enable participants to start making disclosures and share thoughts and experiences

↑ To build trust

↑ To show that everyone is different, and demonstrate that participants may have different viewpoints and experiences to contribute

PREPARATION *materials needed*

Before the session, ask participants to bring along an object that has personal significance for them – something associated with a memory, enjoyed or prized. Examples might be a theatre ticket, a pair of earrings, a book, a CD, a picture, an ornament, a prize won, and so on. Instruct each person that the object must not be shown to other group members and should be given to you so that others will not know what it is.

THE ACTIVITY

The items are laid out on a table. Group members view them, select an item that is not their own and return to their seats, taking care not to damage the item. Group members then, in turn, show the item, guess who it belongs to, and state the reasoning behind their guess. If incorrect, the real person then owns up, states their name and explains what the object means to them.

VARIATION

Simplify the process by having each person introduce themselves, the object they have brought in and what it means to them.

COMMENT

Use the default procedure when group members already know each other slightly and the variation when people are completely new to each other.

USE ALSO FOR

Building trust, energising and motivation.

Goofy questions

PREPARATION *materials needed*

Write some fun questions on card or on pieces of paper. Examples are:

→ Would you rather be a snake or an elephant? Why?

→ Would you rather shave your head or have a tattoo? Why?

→ What historical or fictional character would you like to invite to dinner? Why?

→ Would you rather spend a day in outer space or on the sea bed? Why?

→ If you were a fruit would you be an orange or a pear? Why?

AIMS

↑ To enable participants to get to know each other

↑ To prepare for self-disclosure

↑ To begin building trust

↑ To have fun

↑ To energise group members after a difficult time

THE ACTIVITY

Have group members either view the cards and choose one, or hand them out randomly. Allow a pause for thought and then invite participants, in turn, to state their name, read out the question and answer it.

VARIATION

If participants do not know each other, ask everyone, in turn, to state their name. Ask for a volunteer to read out their question. That person then names someone else to respond and answer it.

COMMENT

Good as a light-hearted introduction or energiser between other activities.

USE ALSO FOR

Building trust, energising and motivation.

Fears and hopes

AIMS

↑ To introduce group members

↑ To help them start working together

↑ To identify fears and expectations

PREPARATION *materials needed*

Prepare sheets of paper with the following sentence beginnings written on them.

1 My name is ...

2 What I fear most about this group is ...

3 What I hope to gain from the group is ...

You will also need to have pens or pencils available.

THE ACTIVITY

Hand out the sheets of paper and invite everyone to complete the sentences. Each person, in turn, then reads out what he or she has written. Participants' fears and what they hope to gain from the group can be written on a flipchart under two headings 'fears' and 'hopes' and discussed with everyone.

VARIATION

Invite participants to state their name and three things they enjoy doing. Ask them to call out, in turn, what they fear about the group; then do another round asking everyone what they hope to gain from it. The 'fears' and 'hopes' are written up on the flipchart and discussed.

COMMENT

If you invite people to write down their fears and hopes as soon as they arrive they then have more time to prepare answers. The flipchart can be shown again at the end of the session and participants asked if their fears were overcome and their hopes realised. This is a gentle introductory exercise to use with people who feel anxious about the group and what might be expected of them.

USE ALSO FOR

Building trust, energising, motivation, stimulating learning and managing behaviour and personal responsibility.

Getting acquainted

PREPARATION *materials needed*

Have some music available to play during the session – either on CD or on tape.

THE ACTIVITY

Ask participants what happens when people first meet and want to get to know each other. Tell them that is what everyone is going to do. Say you are going to play some music and want everyone to walk around the room. When the music stops they introduce themselves to the nearest person and find out at least two things about them. When the music restarts everyone walks about again until the music stops, and they repeat the process. This can be repeated as often as required, or for a set period of time.

VARIATION

Divide the group in two, with an equal number of people in each half. Each sub-group forms a circle, one outer and one inner. When the music starts, one circle walks to the right and the other to the left. When the music stops, people opposite each other introduce themselves, as above. When the music restarts, the circles proceed again in opposite directions.

COMMENT

This activity is good for getting a group started, for getting to know new people, mixing and breaking down barriers. It is also a good method to use to energise participants or split them into pairs. Instead of introducing themselves they can share views on particular topics or on what has been learned in the session. This is an excellent multipurpose activity.

USE ALSO FOR

Building trust, energising and motivation.

Speechmark P This page may be photocopied for instructional use only. The Group Leader's Toolkit © Robin Dynes 2006

↑ To introduce people to each other

↑ To break down barriers

↑ To prepare people to work together

↑ To instil a sense of fun

Things I like

PREPARATION *materials needed*

Have pens, paper and small safety pins or alternatives ready to hand out.

THE ACTIVITY

Give each person paper, a pen and a safety pin. Ask them to write down their name and four or five things they like doing. Typical responses might be:

→ I like walking on sand

→ I like fresh apples

→ I like playing darts

→ I like getting up early in the morning

→ I like the smell of coffee.

Everyone pins their completed statements to their shirt or top and walks around reading each others' 'likes'. They introduce themselves and start chatting about their preferences. After a set time, or when everyone has chatted to everyone else, end the activity.

VARIATION

Use other topics, such as:

→ Things I hate are ...

→ Things I would like to do are ...

→ I am good at ...

→ What I would like to achieve through this session/course/group is ...

→ What I have learned this session is ...

→ What I have got out of the session so far is ...

COMMENT

This is another good multipurpose activity that can be used for a variety of purposes and gets people circulating, interacting and sharing viewpoints.

USE ALSO FOR

Building trust, energising and motivation.

Assets I bring

PREPARATION *materials needed*

None.

THE ACTIVITY

Introduce the activity by saying that everyone brings assets to the group from which it will benefit. Ask everyone to think for a moment and decide what particular asset they bring. They then, in turn, state their name and the asset. Statements might be:

→ My name is Meena; I bring a good sense of humour

→ My name is Bob; I bring enthusiasm

→ My name is Joy; I bring an inquisitive nature

→ My name is Roy; I bring a reflective nature

Participants can, of course, be asked to state more than one asset – or have a second round.

VARIATION

Break the group into pairs or sub-groups of three or four to discuss 'assets' and decide on what they might bring to the group. Ask them to state their names and what they bring to the group as a pair or sub-group.

COMMENT

The variation is best used when people may lack confidence or have difficulty making statements. If a group is becoming despondent or negative use this exercise to change the mood, asking people to make positive statements about themselves. For example: 'Things I do well are …'

USE ALSO FOR

Building trust, energising and motivation.

AIMS

↑ To introduce people to each other

↑ To break down barriers

↑ To encourage a positive attitude

↑ To encourage working together

Memory game

AIMS

↑ To introduce people to each other

↑ To break down barriers

↑ To encourage self-disclosure

↑ To create a sense of fun and enjoyment

PREPARATION *materials needed*

None.

THE ACTIVITY

Ask the group to sit in a circle and ask for a volunteer. This volunteer states his name and something about himself that he does not mind sharing with the group. The player on his right then repeats what the first person has said, states his own name and makes a statement about himself. The person on his right now repeats what participants one and two have said, states his own name and shares his own personal details. This procedure continues round the circle.

VARIATION

The game can be kept simple by merely having participants repeat the names in this manner, or participants may state their name and complete a supplied statement. An example would be: 'I went to a party and took ….' The first player might say: 'I went to a party and took a bottle of wine.' The second participant repeats this and adds an item of their own, and so on. Many useful beginnings can be invented to suit any type of group. Examples might be:

→ I went on holiday and packed …

→ I went to a meeting and took …

→ I went shopping and bought …

COMMENT

An introductory activity that is simple, non-threatening and fun. If participants have difficulty remembering, prompts can be given by other members of the group.

USE ALSO FOR

Building trust, energising and motivation.

Animals

PREPARATION *materials needed*

Have available slips of paper or small cards and pens.

THE ACTIVITY

Give each participant a card and invite each person to write on the card an animal that he thinks would represent him or whose characteristics he shares. When completed, collect and shuffle the cards. A group member then chooses a card at random, and reads out the animal written on it. The group tries to guess who the animal represents. When they have succeeded, that person states his name and a makes a brief statement of the qualities he thinks he shares with the animal.

VARIATION

Instead of animals use flowers, cars, historical characters, buildings, TV characters, food, and so on.

COMMENT

Using pictures of animals, flowers, food or whatever theme chosen – and having participants mix and choose from the selection on a table – can add an element of fun to this activity. Individuals then show the picture chosen and make their statements.

USE ALSO FOR

Building trust, energising and motivation.

 # Question time

AIMS

↑ To introduce people to each other

↑ To break down barriers

↑ To prepare group members to make disclosures

↑ To create a sense of fun and enjoyment

PREPARATION *materials needed*

Prepare slips of paper or cards with a question on each one for each member of the group. Example questions are:

→ What qualities do you respect in others?

→ What have you done or achieved in the past that you are proud of?

→ How would you like to be remembered by your friends after you have died?

→ What would you do if you suddenly came into a lot of money?

→ What annoys or frustrates you about life today?

→ What is your favourite hobby? Why?

→ Who is your favourite author/actor/ singer? Why?

→ If you could choose to live anywhere in the world, where would it be? Why?

→ What do you value and appreciate in life today? Why?

→ If you could choose someone famous to date, who would it be?

THE ACTIVITY

Give each group member a card with a question written on it. Ask them to circulate, speak to each member of the group, ask their names and get an answer to the question they have been given.

VARIATION

Make the questions relevant to the session/group aims etc.

COMMENT

This is a useful introductory exercise. The questions can easily be adapted to fit any group or situation and the cards can be kept to reuse.

USE ALSO FOR

Building trust, energising and motivation.

Who I relate to

PREPARATION *materials needed*

None.

THE ACTIVITY

AIMS

↑ To introduce people to each other

↑ To encourage self-disclosure

↑ To create a relaxed atmosphere

Ask the group members to think about a famous person or fictional character with whom they identified when young. What characteristics did this person have? What was it about this person that they admired? Do they still admire or aspire to these characteristics? Once the participants have had time to think, invite each person to state his name and the name of the famous person or fictional character with whom they identified. Then ask him what he admired and whether or not he sees that quality reflected in himself.

VARIATION

Invite participants to reflect on people in their own lives whom they admired or looked up to – such as a teacher, best friend or aunt.

COMMENT

A good non-threatening introduction that gives participants confidence for further disclosures later.

USE ALSO FOR

Building trust, energising and motivation.

Find the person

AIMS

↑ To introduce group members to each other

↑ To break down barriers

↑ To start people working together

↑ To start building trust

↑ To challenge individuals

↑ To introduce a sense of fun and enjoyment

PREPARATION *materials needed*

Write each participant's name on a label and pair the names up.

THE ACTIVITY

Give out the labels, making sure that you give each participant the label with the name of the person you want them to partner. Now ask people to find the person whose label they have been given, introduce themselves and find out three things about that person. After sufficient time has elapsed to complete the task, each person, in turn, introduces their new-found acquaintance to the whole group.

VARIATIONS

1 Prepare labels with consecutive numbers on, to match the number of people in the group. As people arrive give them a numbered label and ask them to stick it on their shirt or top. Ask even numbers to pair up with odd numbers, find out information about their partner and then introduce each other to the group.

2 Put the numbers in a hat and have people pick them out at random and then proceed as above.

COMMENT

If you have an odd number of people in the group, join in yourself to make an even number. These activities are good ways of dividing a group into pairs and ensuring people do not always pair up with someone they know.

USE ALSO FOR

Building trust, energising and motivation.

Preferences

PREPARATION *materials needed*

Have available a flipchart and magic markers.

THE ACTIVITY

Write the names of the four seasons on a flipchart or board. Ask the group members to state, in turn, their names and which season they prefer, giving the reason. If you want to do more rounds, use colours, types of music, fruits or times of day.

AIMS

↑ To introduce people to each other
↑ To encourage group members to become active participants
↑ To break down barriers
↑ To have fun

VARIATION

Do several rounds with different themes. Record the numbers of people who have the same preferences on the flipchart, and then discuss similarities and differences.

COMMENT

A useful exercise, which can also be used to show and discuss diversity of viewpoints.

USE ALSO FOR

Building trust, energising, motivation and managing behaviour and personal responsibility.

Birthplace

1

AIMS

↑ To introduce people to each other

↑ To break down barriers

↑ To encourage participation

↑ To begin building trust

PREPARATION *materials needed*

Have available cards or paper and pens.

THE ACTIVITY

Ask each person, in turn, to state their name and where they were born and to describe or share one or two facts of interest about their birthplace.

VARIATION

Have participants write down their place of birth on a slip of paper or card. The cards are then placed in a hat and shuffled. Invite group members, in turn, to pick a card at random and read what is on it. Group members then try to guess who was born there. In the process they have to ask each other their names. When the person is discovered, he says or repeats his name and makes a statement about his place of birth.

COMMENT

A gentle exercise that is useful when participants first meet or seem anxious about being asked to participate.

USE ALSO FOR

Building trust, energising and motivation.

Building trust

Activities to help group members build trust, to enable openness and to encourage a sense of mutual support.

2 Differences

AIMS

↑ To build trust

↑ To learn about and accept differences between group members

↑ To encourage a sense of individuality and uniqueness

PREPARATION *materials needed*

None.

THE ACTIVITY

Break the group up into pairs. Ask each pair to discuss the differences between them. Their task is to find at least four areas in which they differ. Emphasise that this should be done in a spirit of valuing and accepting differences, taste, abilities and viewpoints. They might consider:

→ looks

→ what they like

→ what they are good at

→ what they dislike

→ character traits such as being stubborn, easy going and so on

After a few minutes, bring the whole group together and invite each participant to state four ways in which he and his partner differ.

VARIATION

Form sub-groups of three or four people and get each sub-group to discuss differences and explore four things that are different about each person in their group. Stipulate that only one difference can be about appearance.

COMMENT

This exercise encourages group members to value and accept differences and build trust. It also helps to build a sense of the uniqueness of individuals.

USE ALSO FOR

Introductions and icebreaker, energising, stimulating learning, managing behaviour and personal responsibility and assessment and evaluation.

Belief statements

2

PREPARATION *materials needed*

Prepare a number of belief statements, such as:

→ Chocolate is good for you

→ Black cats are lucky

→ You should call a spade a spade

→ Familiarity breeds contempt

→ Men are better drivers than women

→ Absence makes the heart grow fonder

→ Best is cheapest

→ A fool and his money are soon parted

Depending on your objective, you can make the belief statements general, as above, or specific to the subject matter on which you are focussing.

AIMS

↑ To provide physical movement

↑ To begin building trust

↑ To create a sense of fun and enjoyment

↑ To encourage participation

↑ To energise the group

THE ACTIVITY

Put an 'agree' notice at one end of the room and a 'disagree' notice at the other. Read out one of the belief statements and ask those who agree to go to the 'agree' end and those who disagree to the other. Those who are doubtful stay in the middle. Once everyone is satisfied that they are where they want to be, each person states why they have chosen their position. Then read out another belief statement. Continue in this way until all the belief statements have been used.

VARIATION

Instead of belief statements, use likes and dislikes such as 'I like cats', 'I dislike fish', 'I like going to the cinema', and so on. Alternatively, use statements beginning with 'I believe …'. Examples might be: 'I believe the earth is square', 'I believe that I can't cope with change', 'I believe that learning is a waste of time', 'I believe that people go out of their way to be helpful', and so on.

COMMENT

A game that can be used at any time to sharpen participants when they begin to flag, to keep them involved, to encourage participation and to help build trust. Always use non-threatening statements with new groups.

USE ALSO FOR

Energising, stimulating learning and problem solving.

2 Going on a journey

AIMS

↑ To find out individual expectations from the session

↑ To break down barriers

↑ To identify shared interests of group members

↑ To obtain feedback

PREPARATION *materials needed*

You will need some plain cards and pens to hand out to the group members.

THE ACTIVITY

Give a card and a pen to each participant. Tell the group they are going on a journey (a holiday, perhaps) and ask them to think of your session or sessions together as the journey. Ask them to write down their expectations of what they want to do, see and experience. Then ask for volunteers to share their expectations with the group.

At the end of the session or series of sessions the cards can be read out again and people asked to state if their expectations have been met, and how.

VARIATION

Ask participants to write about how they are feeling at the beginning of the group session. This is shared with other group members. Repeat the process again at the end of the session.

COMMENT

Group members who do not want to share what they have written do not have to. At the end of the session, they can simply say whether their expectations have or have not been met.

USE ALSO FOR

Introductions and icebreaker, energising, stimulating learning and problem solving.

Disclosures

PREPARATION *materials needed*

Have available a small soft cushion or other soft object, such as a teddy bear. For the variation (see below) paper and pens will also be required.

THE ACTIVITY

Explain that the group members will pass the cushion from person to person around the group. The participant who has the cushion shares something personal that no-one in the group knows. Emphasise that this disclosure should be something inconsequential, for example: something they did when young, such as breaking an ornament and never owning up to it, or a hobby that they have not spoken about.

VARIATION

Give each participant paper and a pen and ask him to write down a disclosure – something that he does not yet want to share with the group. Then ask if anyone would like to share what he has written. Make sure that everyone understands that it is perfectly acceptable *not* to share. Tell those who do not wish to share that there will be an opportunity to do so later. Provide that opportunity later in the session and ask those who have shared their disclosure if they want to make any further comment but still make it clear that it is fine not to.

COMMENT

Participants who are at first doubtful may later feel more comfortable and able to make their disclosure, though several sessions may pass before they do so. Those who have not made disclosures can destroy their statements or keep them in a sealed envelope and make their disclosure later if they wish.

USE ALSO FOR

Energising, stimulating learning and assessment and evaluation.

AIMS

↑ To build trust to make disclosures
↑ To get to know each other better
↑ To break down barriers
↑ To help people feel safe

2 Feelings

AIMS

↑ To build trust

↑ To start feeling safe when making disclosures

↑ To encourage participants to express their feelings

↑ To provide insight and awareness of self and others

PREPARATION *materials needed*

A flipchart and magic marker will be needed for the variation.

THE ACTIVITY

Each person in the group makes a statement beginning, 'I feel good when …'. This could be, 'I feel good when something I have done well is acknowledged' or, 'I feel good when I can talk things through.' This can then be followed by another round, with statements beginning, 'I feel bad when …'. This could be, 'I feel bad when no one speaks to me' or 'I feel bad when I don't see my son'.

VARIATION

Have the group brainstorm a number of 'feeling' words and write these on the flipchart. Words might include *embarrassed, sad, happy, afraid, confident,* and so on. Invite the group members to make a statement that uses one of these words and begins, 'I feel …'. An example might be, 'I feel happy when I am with people.'

COMMENT

Opportunities can be given to expand on statements made if individuals feel comfortable doing so. Make it clear that a bald statement is acceptable if an individual feels more comfortable with that.

USE ALSO FOR

Introductions and icebreakers, energising, stimulating learning and problem solving.

Grumble time

PREPARATION *materials needed*

Prepare pieces of paper or small cards with 'grumbles' written on them. Grumbles may be general or specific to the group or subject matter. Examples are: dogs, the weather, youth today, teachers, TV soaps, pollution, smokers, shopping centres, violence, sex, vandalism, and so on. A flipchart and magic marker will be needed for the variation.

THE ACTIVITY

Lay the grumbles out on a table and have the group members circulate. Ask each participant to choose one grumble that he can relate to. Participants then explain, one at a time, why they feel their grumble is important and how it has affected them, or might affect them in the future.

VARIATION

Have the group members call out general grumbles or specific grumbles about the group or the session subject. Write these up on the flipchart. Participants, in turn, then choose a grumble and explain why they feel strongly about it.

COMMENT

If you become aware that there is dissatisfaction building in the group about specific issues, this can be a good way of getting them out in the open. If you choose to bring them out you must also help the group members work through these issues, or provide some answers.

USE ALSO FOR

Energising, stimulating learning and problem solving.

AIMS
↑ To build trust
↑ To encourage participants to start making disclosures
↑ To let off steam
↑ To enable dissatisfactions to be aired
↑ To draw out those reluctant to express opinions

 **Treasured memories**

AIMS

↑ To build trust

↑ To encourage participants to start making disclosures

↑ To promote self-awareness

↑ To enable people to get to know each other better

PREPARATION *materials needed*

None.

THE ACTIVITY

Everyone has treasured memories. These may include a special birthday, a holiday, time spent with someone, school, a honeymoon or a particular time of life, such as schooldays. Ask group members to think back to a special time and then ask them, one by one, to describe it briefly and say what made it special.

VARIATION

Ask group members to imagine that they have to leave their home in a hurry because of fire or a flood. They only have time to take a few objects in a small case. What items would they choose? Explore the reasons why the items have been chosen and what each one means to the person.

COMMENT

This is a pleasant exercise that stimulates discussion. Also, it helps group members to begin sharing their thoughts and to build trust in each other.

USE ALSO FOR

Energising and problem solving.

Blind guide

PREPARATION *materials needed*

Provide some strips of material that you can use as blindfolds – one per pair of participants.

THE ACTIVITY

Split the group into pairs and have them decide which of them is 'A' and which is 'B'. Invite them to line up at one end of the room. Have all the 'A' people put the blindfolds on the 'B's. Arrange around the room some large obstacles, such as chairs, tables or other large objects. Avoid small items that people might fall over. Once everything is in place, ask the 'A' people to guide those who are blindfolded, by use of voice only, around the room, helping them to avoid the obstacles. Then all the 'A' people are blindfolded, the furniture is moved to different positions, and the 'A's are guided around the room by the 'B's.

Afterwards, discuss how the participants felt being in control and giving up control to someone else.

VARIATION

For groups who might find the above difficult, have the person who is being a guide spin their partner around three times and then guide their partner around the room without placing obstacles in the way.

COMMENT

This activity can be difficult for some participants and they may need reassurance about their safety.

USE ALSO FOR

Energising, stimulating learning and problem solving.

AIMS

↑ To create an atmosphere of trust
↑ To learn it is safe to let go of control
↑ To experience trusting someone with their physical safety
↑ To experience being trusted with someone's safety

2 Positive qualities

AIMS

↑ To build trust
↑ To remind people about their qualities
↑ To support each other
↑ To boost self-esteem
↑ To provide awareness of how individuals are seen by other people

PREPARATION *materials needed*

You will need pens, pieces or strips of paper and large envelopes. Prepare an envelope for each participant with his name clearly written on it. For the variation you will need a flipchart, magic markers and drawing pins.

THE ACTIVITY

Place the envelopes and strips of paper around the room and instruct the participants to write something positive about each group member – one comment to each strip of paper. They then place the strips of paper in the appropriate envelopes. When everyone has completed the task, hand each envelope to the person named written on it. Everyone then reads what has been written about them. Briefly discuss how people feel about what has been written.

VARIATION

Pin flipchart sheets around the walls of the room. Allocate one sheet for each group member, with his name written at the top. Give out magic markers. Group members then move around the flipcharts writing one positive comment about each person named.

COMMENT

An exercise that makes the group members feel good about themselves and creates a feeling of warmth.

USE ALSO FOR

Energising, stimulating learning and problem solving.

What I am like

2

PREPARATION *materials needed*

Prepare sheets of paper with all the following starter statements written on each one. Each group member requires a sheet.

→ *My name is ...*

→ *What I like most about myself is ...*

→ *What I dislike most about myself is ...*

→ *What I am good at is ...*

→ *An animal (or flower) that represents me is ...*

You should also have pens available.

AIMS

↑ To build trust
↑ To get to know each other better
↑ To encourage participants to start to make disclosures
↑ To raise self-awareness

THE ACTIVITY

Hand out the sheets of paper and instruct participants to complete the sentences. When this has been done, invite each person, in turn, to read aloud what they have written. When each participant has read out his completed statements, discuss them briefly with the group. Do the other group members agree that the chosen animal/flower represents the person?

VARIATION

Use fewer starter statements than given as an example above.

COMMENT

Make the starter statements suit the subject matter of a session or particular themes, for example:

→ My name is …

→ What I like best about my job is …

→ What I dislike most about my job is …

→ What I am good at is …

→ An animal that represents me is …

As shown, this exercise can easily be adapted to prompt discussion concerning relationships or situations.

USE ALSO FOR

Introductions and icebreakers, energising and stimulating learning.

2 Expressing feelings

AIMS

↑ To build trust

↑ To encourage people to express their feelings

↑ To encourage participants to start to make disclosures

PREPARATION *materials needed*

None.

THE ACTIVITY

Briefly discuss some of the changes that occur in life such as leaving home, changing jobs, getting married, the break-up of a relationship, moving house, having a new boss, and so on. Split the group into pairs. Ask each pair to discuss one change that they have experienced. What were they feeling before, during and after the change? Bring the group members together again and ask how they felt expressing their feelings.

VARIATION

As above, discuss various changes that occur in life. Ask group members to think about a change experienced and how they felt about it. After a moment or two, ask for a volunteer to describe a change that he experienced and how he felt before, during and after it. When he has finished, ask for another volunteer until everyone in the group has had a turn.

COMMENT

To make the variation easier ask the participants to write down their experience of change, stating how they felt about it. Invite volunteers to read aloud what they have written. The exercise allows people to discuss something non-threatening and to build the confidence and trust that will enable them to make more personal statements later.

USE ALSO FOR

Energising, stimulating learning and problem solving.

Positive visualisation

PREPARATION *materials needed*

None.

THE ACTIVITY

Ask participants to make themselves comfortable, close their eyes, relax and breathe in and out in an even, easy manner. Tell them to imagine all their tensions draining through their bodies, down their legs and into the ground.

Now ask them to imagine being transported to a relaxing place, beside a river, on a beach, in a garden or anywhere else they find peaceful. Say,

> Imagine that you and all the members of the group are interacting together, doing what feels good and comfortable. Soak up the moment. Let any obstacles that get in the way rise and float to the surface of your mind. Note the difficulty or fear and then let it drift away. Continue to enjoy the experience, safety and company of the group. Enter into the positive feeling of relating in this way. Experience it as if it is completely true and happening now. Touch, smell, hear and feel it. Experience it in detail. Accept it as real and bask in the enjoyment of it.

Pause and let the participants soak up what they are experiencing

> Now look at the experience you have created in your mind. Allow yourself to believe and feel that it is possible to relate in this manner with other members of the group. When you are ready, gradually allow the scene to fade or drift away out of sight. When it has, open your eyes and adjust to being in the group again.

VARIATION

When the group feels that external events are intruding and they are unable to settle down, change some of the above words. Instead of, 'Let any obstacles float to the surface ...', and so on, ask them to let the worry or intruding thought come to mind and then let it drift away. Tell them to imagine themselves cutting out all the world and being embraced by the group.

AIMS
↑ To build trust
↑ To break through any psychological blocks
↑ To reduce anxiety
↑ To help the group relax and bond

COMMENT

This delightful exercise can be adapted to most situations to create a relaxed and comfortable feeling.

USE ALSO FOR

Energising, stimulating learning and problem solving.

Personal flag

PREPARATION *materials needed*

Have available sheets of paper and pencils or crayons to hand out to group members.

THE ACTIVITY

Give each person paper and crayons or a pencil. Ask them to draw a horizontal line in the centre of the sheet and a vertical line so the sheet is divided into four. Each participant numbers the sections in the first row 1, 2, and the sections in the second row 3 and 4. Invite the participants to write their names across the top of the sheet; then ask them to draw a picture and in each section respond to the following statements:

→ Section 1 – How I see myself now

→ Section 2 – What makes me happy

→ Section 3 – Things I am proud of

→ Section 4 – How I would like to be

Make it clear that the drawings can be of matchstick people: good drawing is not expected. When this has been completed ask participants, one at a time, to show their drawings and explain them to the other group members.

VARIATION

Ask the group members to answer each question by using words instead of drawing, or a mixture of both.

COMMENT

Reduce the time taken for this exercise by preparing the sheets so that they are already divided and numbered. It may be necessary or appropriate to change the questions to fit the purpose of the session or group.

USE ALSO FOR

Energising, stimulating learning and problem solving.

AIMS

↑ To build trust

↑ To encourage participants to start making disclosures

↑ To help people get to know each other better

↑ To raise self-awareness

2 Reasons

AIMS

- ↑ To enable the group to bond
- ↑ To prepare for self-disclosure
- ↑ To identify shared interests
- ↑ To establish the needs of individuals
- ↑ To help individuals to contribute to the group
- ↑ To outline the contents of the course/session
- ↑ To enable individuals to see how their needs will be met
- ↑ To ensure that people feel involved and start taking personal responsibility

PREPARATION *materials needed*

A flipchart and magic marker will be needed.

THE ACTIVITY

Split the group members into pairs or small groups. Encourage them to discuss their main reason/s for attending. For example, 'I lack confidence talking to people on social occasions', 'I want to make changes in my life', 'I want to find out …' or 'I want to … but I get anxiety attacks when I go out'. Bring everyone back together and invite each sub-group to tell the others their reasons for coming to the session or course. Summarise the reasons on the flipchart.

Next, go through what has been planned for the session or the complete course. Clarify what will be included and negotiate what else from the identified needs can be included but is not yet covered. It may not be possible to include all options, due to time restraints or other reasons, but group members can decide which needs are most important and ensure that these are met.

VARIATION

Have a general discussion about what people would like included on the course, note this on a flipchart and go through what has been planned. If you cannot include everything in your programme, let the group members decide on what is most important.

COMMENT

If time is limited, the variation takes less time: however, it is less effective in starting people working together and ensuring that everyone makes contributions and disclosures.

USE ALSO FOR

Energising, stimulating learning, problem solving and assessment and evaluation.

Likes and dislikes about groups

PREPARATION *materials needed*

Paper, pens, flipchart and magic marker will be needed.

THE ACTIVITY

Give out paper and pens and ask group members to list five things they like and five things they dislike about groups. Divide a sheet of flipchart paper into two columns and make a list of 'likes' and another of 'dislikes'. Invite everyone to share what they have written, starting with the 'likes'. Then discuss the 'dislikes' and how these can be overcome or turned into positives.

VARIATION

Split into small groups to produce the lists of likes and dislikes.

COMMENT

Working in small groups is the easier option for groups who may be anxious. It also has the advantage of making people work together.

USE ALSO FOR

Energising, stimulating learning and problem solving.

AIMS

↑ To build trust
↑ To enable participants to contribute to the group
↑ To share concerns
↑ To help individuals to recognise that they are not alone with their concerns
↑ To help people feel relaxed and able to contribute openly

Energising

3

Activities designed to revive a group, energise participants and stimulate them to re-engage in an active way. They can be used to get people involved at the start of a session or in the first few meetings of a group – or when attention and interest are waning.

3 Exercise break

AIMS

↑ To re-energise group members

↑ To instil a sense of fun

↑ To get people moving after a long period spent sitting down

↑ To change the mood in the group

PREPARATION *materials needed*

None.

THE ACTIVITY

Have a few physical exercises, movements or tasks in mind for the group. Examples might be, running or walking on the spot, walking in a clockwise direction around the room, stopping to chat to the person nearest to you, waving your hands above your head, bending your knees three times, standing on one leg, and so on. Once you have given two or three instructions, ask group members in turn to shout out an exercise or instruction. Continue in this manner for about five minutes.

VARIATION

Do a round of 'Simon says'. (Simon says 'wave your arms', Simon says 'raise your left arm', and so on.) Explain that everyone has to do the actions. Give the commands in quick succession. If a command is given without the prefix 'Simon says …', anyone who does the action is out. When only one person is left, he takes over as the person giving the orders. Continue for about five minutes.

COMMENT

This is a familiar game which can be made vigorous or gentle to suit the abilities of participants. It is fun, and it helps participants to concentrate.

USE ALSO FOR

Problem solving and closures.

Scramble

PREPARATION *materials needed*

Make four or more lists of between five and 10 items to be looked for and found. Examples might be: a hairbrush, the fire extinguisher on your premises, a blue scarf, a bus ticket, a newspaper, a ruler. These can be items found in the room or building in which the activity takes place, brought in by you, or a mixture of both. Place the items around the building or room before the session starts.

AIMS

↑ To energise group members
↑ To explore members' resourcefulness
↑ To help people relax
↑ To have fun

THE ACTIVITY

Divide the group into four or more teams. Give each team a list and instruct them to find the items. Set a time by which everyone has to be back. See which team has found the most items.

VARIATION

Instead of using lists of items, set simple tasks to do. Examples might be to give each team a copy of a crossword to complete, to get them to work out a maths problem or to complete a poem.

COMMENT

This is a light-hearted activity that encourages people to work together. Small prizes can be given to the winning team, such as a bookmark each or a bar of chocolate.

USE ALSO FOR

Motivation and managing behaviour and personal responsibility.

3 Shuffle time

AIMS

↑ To energise group members

↑ To encourage people to work together

↑ To have fun

PREPARATION *materials needed*

Obtain copies of a magazine that will appeal to your group. Ensure that the magazine has a contents list. Remove all the page numbers, then cut out and shuffle the pages.

THE ACTIVITY

Split the group into teams. Give each team a copy of the shuffled magazine pages. The task is to sort the pages into the correct order. The first team to complete the task correctly is the winner. When completed have a brief discussion about how the activity felt, who took the lead and who was less involved. Did everyone work as a team? If not, why not?

VARIATION

Instead of magazines, use a report or some other type of document. A small prize can be given to the winning team.

COMMENT

This is a quick fun game that provides an opportunity for people to explore the advantages of working as a team.

USE ALSO FOR

Stimulating learning and motivation.

Puzzler

PREPARATION *materials needed*

Paste a large poster onto card and cut it into puzzle pieces. For groups of 10 people you will need 40 pieces. Mix the pieces up in a bag or a box. Ensure that you have a large table available.

THE ACTIVITY

Give each group member four puzzle pieces, or have them select them at random; then instruct participants to put the puzzle together. Afterwards, have a brief discussion about how it felt doing the puzzle as a group. Who took the lead and who was less involved?

VARIATION

Split the group into teams. Use a smaller puzzle for each group and follow the same procedure.

COMMENT

Team games, as well as being fun, can reveal the roles that people take. Describe and discuss these roles to raise awareness of the roles people adopt in life.

USE ALSO FOR

Introductions and icebreakers, stimulating learning and managing behaviour and personal responsibility.

3 What is it?

AIMS

↑ To energise group members

↑ To break down barriers

↑ To encourage each person to participate

↑ To encourage creative thinking

↑ To have fun

PREPARATION *materials needed*

Have available a ruler, a box, or a biscuit tin.

THE ACTIVITY

Arrange the seating in a circle. Inform the group members that you will be passing a ruler around and request that each person mimes using the ruler as something else. Demonstrate by pretending to use the ruler as a cricket bat or some other implement: the group members must guess what the ruler represents. When they have guessed, the ruler is passed on to the next group member, who mimes using it as a different object. Participants are not allowed to repeat any previous mime. This can be continued round the circle as many times as people can keep the process going or for as long as time allows.

VARIATION

Instead of using a ruler, work with an object such as a box or a biscuit tin. Make a comment about the box: for example, 'This box is square'. It is then passed on to the next person, who makes another comment. Statements must not be repeated.

COMMENT

The participants may keep this going for a long time before they run out of ideas. To make the variation harder, use a ball.

USE ALSO FOR

Stimulating learning.

Object lists

PREPARATION *materials needed*

Have available pens and paper. A flipchart and magic marker will be needed for the variation.

THE ACTIVITY

Split the group members into pairs or small teams. Give out pens and paper. Ask each team to produce a list of items that are made of glass. Allow two or three minutes and then ask how many items each team has thought of. If time allows, have participants write another list. For example, objects that have handles.

AIMS

↑ To energise group members
↑ To break down barriers
↑ To encourage each person to participate
↑ To activate the mind
↑ To encourage sharing ideas
↑ To have fun

VARIATION

Have participants produce lists of types of objects of their own choosing, and then share ideas as a group by writing them on a flipchart.

COMMENT

Many other lists can be requested, such as objects that are bigger than a house, are smaller than a matchbox, are round, grow on trees, make a noise, and so on. The list is endless!

USE ALSO FOR

Building trust.

3 Success celebration

AIMS

↑ To boost morale when group members are feeling low

↑ To energise everyone

↑ To encourage a positive attitude

PREPARATION *materials needed*

None.

THE ACTIVITY

Ask the group members to reflect on three of their greatest successes in life. This could be a sporting achievement, having a child, loyalty, giving support to someone or gaining a qualification. After a pause for reflection, invite each person in the group, in turn, to share his successes.

VARIATION

Do a round of 'The best experience in my life' or 'The happiest moment in my life'.

COMMENT

This activity can also be completed in pairs or small groups. It is a good morale booster.

USE ALSO FOR

Building trust and closures.

Spot the lie

PREPARATION *materials needed*

None

THE ACTIVITY

Ask each group member to state three things about himself – one of which is a lie. The other group members guess which statement is false and explain why they think so. The person who made the statement verifies this or reveals which other item is untrue.

VARIATION

Have participants make a statement that sounds unlikely, such as:

→ I married the same person twice

→ I met Prince Charles in Dorchester in 1985

→ I sang a duet with Elton John

Group members have to vote on whether or not they think the statement is true, and state why they think so.

COMMENT

This activity is great fun. It can also be used as an introductory activity if you ask people to say their name when making their statements.

USE ALSO FOR

Introductions and icebreakers and building trust.

AIMS

↑ To energise group members
↑ To enable people to get to know each other better
↑ To have fun

3 Surprise bag

AIMS

AIMS

↑ To energise group members

↑ To encourage everyone to participate

↑ To encourage a sense of fun

PREPARATION *materials needed*

Prepare some cards or slips of paper, with one task written on each. You need one card for each member of the group. Tasks might be:

→ Lead the group in a one minute jogging-on-the-spot session

→ Lead the group in a two minute session of 'Simon says …'

→ Ask three group members to state something they like and something they dislike

→ Propose a toast

→ Ask group members to pass a compliment to the person on their left

THE ACTIVITY

Hand out the cards at random or ask group members to choose a card from a deck. Make sure that you have a card left for yourself. Start the activities by doing the first task yourself and then continue round the group in turn.

VARIATION

Ask group members, in turn, to lead the group in an activity of their choice for one minute. Give some examples of what they could do.

COMMENT

A fun way of encouraging the involvement of people who are reluctant to contribute, as well as getting minds active again after an information-giving presentation.

USE ALSO FOR

Motivation.

Alphabet game

PREPARATION *materials needed*

Have a list of topics ready, such as place names, countries, flowers, trees, animals, fish, first names, family names, and so on. Pens and paper will be needed.

AIMS

↑ To energise the group
↑ To encourage working as a group
↑ To have fun

THE ACTIVITY

Divide everyone into teams and hand out a pen and paper to each team. Call out a letter of the alphabet and a topic. Within a set time each team must write down as many words as possible beginning with that letter. The team with the most words wins the round. You then announce another letter and topic, and follow the same procedure. Keep this going as long as is appropriate.

VARIATION

At the head of each sheet of paper write a topic and a letter of the alphabet. Hand one sheet out to each group member. Participants list as many words as possible in a set time. The list is then passed to the person on the right and they continue the list for another set period of time. No words can be repeated. See which list is longest at the end.

COMMENT

Group members can also be asked to write words associated with the topics covered during the session.

USE ALSO FOR

Building trust and motivation.

3 How observant are you?

AIMS

↑ To energise group members

↑ To encourage people to mix

↑ To help participants get to know each other better

↑ To encourage everyone to participate

↑ To have fun

PREPARATION *materials needed*

Prepare a list of question, such as:

⇒ What is the name of the person you were talking to?

⇒ Is he wearing jewellery?

⇒ What colour clothes is he wearing?

⇒ What colour are his eyes?

⇒ What colour is his hair?

⇒ What colour are his shoes?

⇒ Is he wearing glasses?

THE ACTIVITY

Ask the group members to pair up with someone they do not know very well. Invite them to introduce themselves to each other and spend two minutes talking about whatever they like. When the time is up, ask people to stand or sit back to back with their partner. They must not look at each other. Now, one at a time, ask the questions you have prepared. See how many people know the answers.

VARIATION

Halfway through a session, have people pair up with someone they have recently met and got to know a little. Have them stand back to back and then ask the questions. See how well they know each other.

COMMENT

This activity gets people moving physically and mentally and helps them to mix, while also having a good time.

USE ALSO FOR

Building trust, motivation and stimulating learning.

Quick change

PREPARATION *materials needed*

None.

THE ACTIVITY

Ask everyone to sit in a circle. Sit on your chair in the centre of the circle. Ask everyone with blue eyes to change chairs. When someone moves, you take their place in the circle. The person left without a chair has to sit in the middle. This person then makes another statement, such as, 'Everyone who has had a holiday this year change chairs', or 'Everyone wearing black shoes change chairs'. Each time, the person without a chair goes in the middle. Continue as long as desired.

VARIATION

Without placing a chair in the middle, have each group member, in turn, make a statement of who will change chairs. Those people then change and another group member makes another statement until everyone has had the opportunity to say who will change chairs.

COMMENT

A fun energiser that relieves stress and gets everyone activated and refreshed.

USE ALSO FOR

Building trust and stimulating learning.

AIMS
↑ To energise group members
↑ To involve everyone in an active way
↑ To encourage people to move position in the room
↑ To have fun

3 Identify the plant

AIMS

↑ To energise group members

↑ To encourage people to mix

↑ To allow everyone to move around

↑ To have fun

PREPARATION *materials needed*

Obtain a number of different plant bulbs, put them in transparent bags and number the bags. Make a careful list of the numbers and the plant names. Pens and paper will be needed.

THE ACTIVITY

Lay the numbered transparent bags on a table or around the room. Give each group member a sheet of paper and a pen. Announce how many bags there are and ask participants to circulate and write what plant they think each bulb originates from. When everyone has completed the task, go through the list and see who has got the most correct answers.

VARIATION

To make the activity easier, prepare a list of the plants; the task is to match each plant listed with the correct numbered bag.

COMMENT

When selecting the bulbs, try to provide as wide a variation as possible, for example, daffodil, snowdrop, onion, garlic, lily, amaryllis, gladioli, fennel, hyacinth, iris, cyclamen and tulip.

USE ALSO FOR

Introductions and icebreakers.

Avoidance

3

PREPARATION *materials needed*

None.

THE ACTIVITY

Ask for a volunteer. The other participants fire questions at him, trying to elicit a 'yes' or 'no' answer. The volunteer tries to avoid these words in his answer. Answers will be statements such as, 'I did', 'I enjoyed that', 'I am 25 years old' or 'I love the taste'. If the volunteer says either of the forbidden words, or the prescribed time limit is reached, he rejoins the group and another volunteer takes a turn. Continue in this manner until everyone in the group has had the opportunity to volunteer.

VARIATION

Divide the group into two teams. Label one team 'A' and the other team 'B'. A member of team 'A' answers questions from team 'B' until someone says the forbidden words. A member of team 'B' then answers questions from team 'A', and so on. The team whose member lasts the longest without saying 'yes' or 'no' wins the round. Continue until everyone has participated.

COMMENT

A simple game that entertains and enlivens the group.

USE ALSO FOR

Building trust.

AIMS

↑ To energise group members
↑ To help people relax
↑ To have fun

3 Going through the motions

AIMS

↑ To energise group members

↑ To involve all the participants

↑ To incorporate physical movement

↑ To add a sense of fun

PREPARATION *materials needed*

None.

THE ACTIVITY

Invite the group to form a circle. Start the activity by demonstrating a movement, such as waving goodbye, tapping a foot or scratching your head. The person on your right then performs your movement and adds one of his own. The person after that repeats both movements and adds a third and so on round the circle, until everyone has participated.

VARIATION

It can be more fun if all the participants who have performed movements do all the actions together each time. Then the person whose turn it is adds their own movement. Eventually everyone is in motion together.

COMMENT

Movements can be simple or energetic, depending on the abilities of people in the group.

USE ALSO FOR

Building trust.

Stimulating learning

Techniques and activities that will stimulate learning in different groups. The activities can be used to vary a programme.

4 Collaboration

AIMS

↑ To help people to learn from and accept support from others
↑ To instigate collaboration
↑ To promote cooperation
↑ To strengthen interpersonal skills and decision making
↑ To encourage the shouldering of responsibility

PREPARATION *materials needed*

Prepare descriptions of scenarios, problems and dilemmas for the group members to discuss and reach some conclusions and decisions about. Ensure that the mix of prompts is appropriate to the group goals. Examples might be:

1 Each person has to purchase a new car. What would influence your decision on which car to purchase?

2 What is an 'ideal' marriage?

3 You are working on a project. The person with whom you are supposed to be working keeps putting off meetings that you arrange. You feel angry and frustrated. What would you do?

You should also provide a large sheet of paper and a magic marker for each sub-group.

THE ACTIVITY

Divide the participants into sub-groups. Present each sub-group with a scenario to discuss, a problem to solve, a decision to make, an action plan to work out, or options to choose from.

Give the group a set time to complete the task and write their conclusions on a large sheet of paper. Then bring the group together again. Have each sub-group read out their scenario or task, explain their conclusions and defend them against any questions from other group participants.

Close the exercise by discussing the process and benefits of collaborating with others to reach a shared decision.

VARIATION

If the group is not too big, go through the process together, as one group.

COMMENT

This is an excellent exercise for highlighting the benefits of sharing problems or working collaboratively as a means to producing creative solutions.

USE ALSO FOR

Energising, motivation and managing behaviour and personal responsibility.

Discover the question

4

PREPARATION *materials needed*

Prepare a number of cards. Write on each one something that participants have learned in a previous session, for example: a strategy, a process, a definition or how to use a piece of equipment. Here are three random examples taken from a session on developing a healthy lifestyle:

1 A healthy lifestyle incorporates sensible exercise, diet and leisure.

2 It is recommended that everyone participates in at least 30 minutes of moderate-intensity activities on at least five days each week.

3 When under stress, everyone's digestive system slows down.

AIMS

↑ To revise learning

↑ To improve deductive thinking

↑ To practise focused questioning

THE ACTIVITY

Invite a group member to pick a card ensuring that no one else sees what is written on it. Encourage other group members to ask questions to find out what is written on the card. The person holding the card may only respond with 'yes' or 'no'. When the process of questioning has revealed the item on the card, another group member selects a card and the process begins again. This continues until every learning point on the cards has been identified.

VARIATIONS

1 Prepare three or four decks of cards with learning points written on them and form three or four sub-groups; instruct each sub-group to proceed as above. This is a useful strategy if the group is large.

2 Stick a card from the pack on the back of each group member. Encourage the participants to circulate asking one question of each other participant until they have discovered what is written on their card.

COMMENT

This is a light-hearted and fun way to revise learning. If done at the end of a session, it leaves everyone feeling good.

USE ALSO FOR

Energising, motivation and assessment and evaluation.

4 On the move

AIMS

↑ To reinforce learning by repetition

↑ To maximise participation

↑ To encourage working with others at random

↑ To help people gain confidence in discussing topics

↑ To make learning fun

PREPARATION *materials needed*

Have a ready list of learning points or topics for discussion.

THE ACTIVITY

Ask the group members to form an inner and an outer circle, with an equal number of people in each. Ask the participants in the inner circle to face those in the outer circle. Introduce the first topic, which the participants then discuss with the person opposite them. After a few minutes, stop the conversations and ask the inner circle to move around until told to stop. The previous discussion is then summarised by the new partners, and any additional points are added. Then tell the outer circle to move on until told to stop, and repeat the process. Repeat several times as appropriate and then introduce another learning point or topic.

VARIATION

Ask the group members to form pairs. Introduce the topic as previously. After one or two minutes ask the group members to walk separately around the room until told to stop. They then pair up with whoever is standing closest to them. Continue as described above.

COMMENT

At the end of the discussion on each topic, have a brief discussion as a complete group before moving on to the next topic.

USE ALSO FOR

Energising and motivation.

Question and answer

PREPARATION *materials needed*

Decide what issues you want the activity to cover. A flipchart and magic marker will be needed.

THE ACTIVITY

Introduce the topic for the activity. Next have the group members brainstorm as many questions as possible about the topic – and write these on the flipchart. Add some questions yourself, if necessary, to ensure all the issues are covered. Take the questions one at a time, asking the group to discuss them and provide the answers. If time is limited, focus on selected issues only.

VARIATION

Form three or four sub-groups and divide the questions between them. For a set time, the groups then discuss and answer the questions they have been given. Each sub-group then summarises its answers and presents them to the complete group.

COMMENT

Invariably, when someone can frame a question they have some ideas about the answer. This activity encourages participants to reflect and appreciate the value of posing questions in the learning process.

USE ALSO FOR

Energising, motivation and assessment and evaluation.

AIMS
- ↑ To encourage participants to ask questions
- ↑ To enable group members to answer their own questions
- ↑ To encourage exploration of topics

4 Reflections

AIMS
- ↑ To stimulate reflective thinking
- ↑ To learn from past experience
- ↑ To encourage creative thinking
- ↑ To encourage risk taking

PREPARATION *materials needed*

None.

THE ACTIVITY

Explain that learning often means taking risks, reflecting on what happens then correcting any mistakes or improving on what has been achieved. Divide the participants into sub-groups and ask them to think about and discuss with each other:

→ A mistake they made in the past and what they learned from it

→ A risk they took in the past and what they learned from it

After a set time invite the sub-groups to feed back their experiences and what they have learned from them to the whole group.

VARIATION

Introduce the topic as above, but do not split the group into sub-groups. Instead give time for reflection; then ask for a volunteer to disclose a mistake he has made, a risk he took and what he learned from doing so. When this person has finished, ask for another volunteer. Continue in this way until everyone has contributed.

COMMENT

This activity makes the participants aware that they are not alone in making mistakes and encourages them to view mistakes as a positive part of the learning process rather than as an embarrassment.

USE ALSO FOR

Energising, motivation and problem solving.

Learning with other people

PREPARATION *materials needed*

Prepare for each participant a rating chart similar to the example on page 62. You may wish to add to or change the issues listed, depending on the type of group. Have available some coloured crayons.

THE ACTIVITY

Hand out the rating chart (one per person) and ask all the participants to rate themselves individually. Make it clear that they need to be honest and that no-one will see their rating unless they wish to share it. When they have finished, lead a discussion on the importance of each issue listed, exploring difficulties and how these can be overcome. Finish by getting everyone to rate themselves again, using a different coloured pen. Discuss any differences in ratings.

AIMS

↑ To prepare participants to work together effectively
↑ To raise awareness of what contributes to group learning
↑ To encourage participants to support each others' learning
↑ To make everyone aware of their personal responsibility for their own and each others' learning

VARIATION

Have each person rate themselves on the first issue listed on the form; then discuss it. After the discussion, invite the participants to rate themselves a second time using a different coloured pen – and see if there is any change. Discuss any differences in ratings. Then go through all the issues in this manner.

COMMENT

This is a useful exercise to use early in the life of a group or when the group members are not working well together.

USE ALSO FOR

Motivation, problem solving and managing behaviour and personal responsibility.

LEARNING WITH OTHER PEOPLE
Rating chart

	1 Poor	2 Fair	3 OK	4 Good	5 Very Good
Appreciating what other people have to offer					
Listening to what other people say					
Speaking in groups					
Preparing for a session					
Putting learning into practice					
Accepting support from others					
Providing support for others					
Dealing with difficulties or unfairness in a group					
Contributing to sessions					
Sharing experience and knowledge					

Reflective logs

PREPARATION *materials needed*

Prepare a simple form and provide pens so that group members may complete it. It should contain spaces for the following items to be written in:

→ Describe the skill/process being practised

→ The situation

→ What happened

→ The outcome

→ How could I improve the skill in a similar situation?

THE ACTIVITY

Hand out the forms (one per participant) and ask the group members to think of a skill or process that they have practised in the past. This could be anything from dealing with a difficult situation to completing a task. It might be something that did not go well or something they would like to improve on. Once everyone has finished writing, ask for volunteers to share what they have written with the group. Other group members may be able to offer further suggestions on how the skill or process could be improved in a similar situation.

VARIATION

Pair up the group members and have them discuss a skill or process that they have practised following the same statements. Each pair then shares with the group the issue that they have discussed.

COMMENT

Writing helps participants to derive maximum benefit from the reflective process. If the activity is used with anyone who has difficulty in writing they could use a tape recorder instead to record their reflections.

USE ALSO FOR

Motivation and problem solving.

AIMS

↑ To encourage reflection when practising skills

↑ To enable participants to learn from experience

↑ To provide a tool for lifelong learning

4 Role play

AIMS

↑ To practise a skill
↑ To rehearse putting an action into practice
↑ To build confidence
↑ To gain insight into behaviour
↑ To explore different options
↑ To explore the effects of actions or behaviours

PREPARATION *materials needed*

Role plays that are prepared in advance tend to address common situations and may not match group members' experience. If time permits it is better to identify from group members' own experience situations that they find difficult. Remember that the purpose is not to reinvent the real situation but to look at what happens in similar situations.

Ensure that trust has been built between group members before attempting role plays.

A video camera and player will be required for the variation.

THE ACTIVITY

Identify situations from the participants' own experience, to use as starting points. Explain the ground rules, which, for example, might include: no yelling, no touching, a signal to stop the role play if anyone feels uncomfortable and a reminder about confidentiality. Emphasise that the point is not to 'get it right' but to explore, practise or rehearse responses to a situation so that participants are better equipped to handle it in the future. Invite participants to play whichever role they feel comfortable with; taking a major role can be risky and stressful.

Once everyone has been briefed on the role play and is clear about the purpose, set the situation and let it happen. Role plays are unpredictable and you should allow them to take their own course. However, be attentive to what is happening and enforce any safeguards necessary to keep everyone safe. Either make notes yourself, for use later in discussion, or encourage group members who are acting as observers to do so.

Do not allow the role play to continue for too long. Five or 10 minutes is usually long enough to bring out the required learning points. A time limit can be set beforehand, or you or the players can decide at what point to bring it to an end.

When the role play has finished, ask all the participants how their character feels 'in role' at that point. The players then need to be debriefed; for example, you might consider:

⇒ Debriefing in a different room

⇒ Asking people to state their name and what they are going to do after the session

⇒ Splitting people into pairs and have them talk about their family, a hobby or what they have planned for the rest of the day

Finally, discuss the role play with both players and observers. Analyse what happened and why, and decide what could have been done to change the outcome. This examination should take much longer than the role play itself.

VARIATION

Obtain participants' permission to video or DVD the role play. The video can then be used for discussion afterwards. Let the group know that the recording will be erased afterwards.

COMMENT

Although role play requires considerable preparation and is time-consuming, it is a powerful learning technique.

USE ALSO FOR

Energising, motivation and problem solving.

4 Event analysis

AIMS

↑ To enable participants to learn from experience

↑ To provide a method of analysing what has happened

↑ To learn how to examine alternative options

↑ To provide a method of achieving a different outcome in the future

PREPARATION *materials needed*

Write the questions below on a flipchart or provide sheets of paper with the process tasks outlined for group members to write on. The questions are:

1 How would you describe the event?

2 What contributed to what happened?

3 What skills are needed to respond to the event?

4 In what alternative ways could the event have been dealt with?

5 How would you respond to a similar event in the future?

A flipchart and magic marker or pens and handout will be needed.

THE ACTIVITY

Form small sub-groups. Instruct each sub-group to choose a difficult event or incident that has happened to one of them away from the group, describe and discuss it using the questions provided. When each sub-group has completed the task, ask it to present its event and findings to the whole group. The larger group comments on each presentation and adds useful suggestions.

A flipchart and magic marker or pens and handout will be needed.

VARIATION

Instead of using actual experiences, prepare a fictional case study for each sub-group to work on.

COMMENT

It can be useful to use fictional case studies first and then repeat the exercise using personal experiences. Bear in mind that trust between participants must be well established before they feel able to discuss their personal experiences.

USE ALSO FOR

Problem solving and managing behaviour and personal responsibility.

What would you do if ...?

PREPARATION *materials needed*

Have ready a series of 'What would you do if ...' questions, such as:

→ What would you do if your boss was taking unfair advantage?

→ What would you do if your best friend broke a confidence?

→ What would you do if you discovered your best friend had stolen something?

→ What would you do if a workmate asked you to lie for her?

Pen and paper or a large sheet of paper and a magic marker will be required for each sub-group.

AIMS

↑ To encourage use of decision-making skills
↑ To encourage the sharing of ideas and options for tackling problems
↑ To reinforce learning
↑ To build confidence

THE ACTIVITY

Divide the group into sub-groups. Provide each sub-group with pen and paper and a 'What would you do if ...?' question to discuss and reach a conclusion about. After a set time invite each sub-group to present its findings and get feedback from the larger group.

VARIATION

Many of the conclusions reached can be followed up with role plays of the scenarios.

COMMENT

This activity is particularly useful for assertiveness, personal relationship and other communication skills groups. It can also be used to discuss a variety of subjects.

USE ALSO FOR

Problem solving and managing behaviour and personal responsibility.

4 Coloured cards

AIMS

↑ To provide opportunities for participants to signal a response

↑ To enable the group leader to know when further explanation/ clarification is needed

↑ To provide a spot check on understanding

↑ To encourage personal responsibility for learning

↑ To make it easy to participate

PREPARATION *materials needed*

Have available sets of red, amber and green cards.

THE ACTIVITY

Give each participant three cards, coloured red, amber and green. Tell them that if at any time they do not understand what is happening or being said or they disagree, they should hold up the red card. If they are losing the thread they should hold up the amber card. If they understand, they should hold up the green card. Every now and then the group leader stops the proceedings and asks for a show of cards – or individuals can show a card at any time. Whatever is causing the problem is repeated, explained in another way or dealt with differently.

VARIATION

Agreed hand signals or different objects for signalling will work instead of cards if you prefer.

COMMENT

This process makes it acceptable not to understand everything and encourages participation. It is ideal for use in meetings, particularly with group members who have a learning disability.

USE ALSO FOR

Building trust and assessment and evaluation.

Information exchange

PREPARATION *materials needed*

Prepare information sheets on your chosen topics; for example, for a session on dealing with conflict one information sheet may contain the following information:

Conflicts can arise from:

→ *wants and needs that are not being met*

→ *fears*

→ *misunderstandings*

→ *lack of trust*

→ *feelings of being controlled or wanting to control someone*

→ *a clash of values, beliefs or boundaries*

Other information sheets on conflict might contain various steps or strategies with which to deal with it. You will need a different sheet for each sub-group. Also provide pens and paper for participants to make notes.

AIMS

↑ To provide information for group members

↑ To ensure that information is learned and understood

↑ To provide information in an interesting way

↑ To ensure that everyone participates

THE ACTIVITY

Make sure each person has a pen and paper on which to make notes. Form sub-groups and give each one an information sheet. Each sub-group reads through its sheet, discusses the information and makes sure that all participants understand it. Each group then sends a visitor to each of the other groups to have their information explained and to ask questions about it. Visitors should make notes if necessary. This process continues until each person has visited all the groups.

VARIATION

Have each sub-group prepare a case study based on the information they are given. Each sub-group then presents their case study to members of the larger group, who ask questions about it.

COMMENT

This activity helps to make interesting the provision of information and actively involves participants.

USE ALSO FOR

Energising, motivation and problem solving.

4 Debate

AIMS

↑ To encourage learning from each other

↑ To involve participants actively in the learning process

↑ To help individuals to question and form opinions

↑ To encourage the testing and owning of learning material

↑ To encourage reflection

↑ To enable participants to apply learning to their own situations

PREPARATION *materials needed*

None.

THE ACTIVITY

After providing learning material during a session, ask the group members to question and debate the topic. This can be done by dividing the group into two teams. Have one team raise anxieties and queries and the other team answer on each issue. Alternatively, form sub-groups to discuss the issues and then feed back their comments and conclusions to the whole group.

VARIATION

Introduce the relevant issues one by one and have the group members discuss each one in relation to their own experience. Keep the debate focused and add any learning points that have not been covered.

COMMENT

Discussion helps participants to apply insights and encourages reflection, and gives them the opportunity to think creatively about related aspects. It also helps individuals to place the learning gained in perspective alongside their other knowledge and skills.

USE ALSO FOR

Energising, motivation, problem solving and managing behaviour and personal responsibility.

Step at a time

PREPARATION *materials needed*

Break down into easy steps a process, a task, or something that has to be learned. Have pens and paper available.

THE ACTIVITY

The group is given a task to complete, a problem to solve or a decision to make; for example, cooking lunch, how to overcome a fear of something or deciding where to go on an outing. Group members are then split into sub-groups. The sub-group members are each assigned a step in the process that will lead them to complete the task. These steps can be numbered if they are to be completed in a particular order. For example, the steps involved in solving a problem might be:

1 State the problem
2 Brainstorm possible solutions
3 Explore the options (advantages and disadvantages)
4 Decide on the best option or combination of options
5 Work out a step-by-step plan of action

When each sub-group has completed its task, bring the whole group back together; discuss what happened in each sub-group and how it felt.

VARIATION

If the process is already known to the group members from previous learning, the steps should not be numbered. Let the group members decide the order in which they should proceed.

COMMENT

Most people enjoy solving problems as presented here. The activity also encourages group members to take responsibility for their own learning.

USE ALSO FOR

Motivation and problem solving.

AIMS

↑ To explain a process
↑ To ensure everyone contributes
↑ To encourage participants to think for themselves
↑ To use problem-solving skills
↑ To make learning experiential
↑ To reinforce previous learning

Demonstrations

AIMS

↑ To show how something is done

↑ To provide an opportunity for people to view a procedure or skill, prior to doing it themselves

↑ To build confidence

↑ To provide material for discussion

PREPARATION *materials needed*

Work out what you are going to do to ensure that all the desired learning points are incorporated; for example, this may be to demonstrate good listening or assertiveness skills, how to use a machine safely or how to guide someone who is blind. It is helpful to have a rehearsal to ensure that your plan is practical and workable. Pens and paper for participants to make notes will be required.

THE ACTIVITY

Outline the learning points and inform the group members that you are going to demonstrate the points. Ask them to take notes for discussion afterwards. Ensure that everyone is able to see and hear what you are doing and begin the demonstration. Afterwards, discuss any issues highlighted and answer questions. It may be helpful, if safe and appropriate, to then invite group members to have a go.

VARIATION

1 Have the more confident group members do the demonstration while the others watch.

2 Demonstrate using incorrect methods, to highlight what can go wrong.

COMMENT

Demonstrations can be used to illustrate behaviours, a skill or present case studies; watching demonstrations may be the favoured learning style for some participants. Although the level of group participation is low, demonstrations can be helpful in building up the confidence of group members who are taking part in doing role plays or practising a skill.

USE ALSO FOR

Motivation and problem solving.

Motivation

Activities and techniques to motivate participants to become and stay involved.

5 What motivates me?

AIMS

↑ To increase self awareness

↑ To assist group members to motivate themselves

↑ To make participants aware of how they can support each other

↑ To encourage taking responsibility for their own success

PREPARATION *materials needed*

A flipchart, magic markers, pens and paper will be required. Large sheets of paper will be needed for the variation.

THE ACTIVITY

Brainstorm with the group what motivates people. Contributions might include:

→ being organised

→ knowing why I'm doing something

→ knowing how I'm going to benefit from doing something

→ having a clear goal in mind

→ money

→ knowing my contribution is appreciated

→ being given deadlines

→ competition

→ being able to discuss things with others

→ constant feedback

When a long list has been written up on the flipchart, have individuals write down a list of five things that help to motivate them personally. When this has been completed, form sub-groups and ask each one to discuss what participants can do to motivate themselves and how the group leader and others can support them.

Conclude the activity by bringing everyone back together as a large group. Discuss what will be gained if everyone takes responsibility for their own motivation and supports others at the same time.

VARIATION

Form sub-groups and have them write a list of 'What motivates me' on a flipchart sheet. The sub-groups then share their lists with the larger group and discuss how they can best motivate themselves and what the group leader and others can do to help.

COMMENT

Some actions that motivate people could be added to any group ground rules agreed by the group. If the group ground rules are on display for each session individuals will be reminded of how they may best support others.

USE ALSO FOR

Energising and managing behaviour and personal responsibility.

What is stopping me?

PREPARATION *materials needed*

Flipchart, magic marker, pens and paper are needed.

THE ACTIVITY

Brainstorm with the group the types of things that kill motivation. These may include:

- laziness
- being bullied
- not wanting to be noticed
- not being organised
- not knowing the purpose of the group
- fear of failure
- not facing problems
- expecting to do everything perfectly
- poor time management
- wanting to be the centre of attention
- being negative
- ignoring the truth

AIMS

- To motivate the group members
- To raise awareness of what kills motivation
- To remove blocks to achieving
- To increase self-awareness

When a substantial list of motivation killers has been written up on the flipchart, give out pens and paper and ask group members to list five points that particularly apply to them. When they have done so, form small groups and invite participants to plan methods of overcoming their motivation killers.

Finally, bring everyone back together as a large group and discuss what will be gained if these motivation killers are eliminated or controlled.

VARIATION

Form small sub-groups and have them write on a flipchart sheet a list of 'Factors that will stop me succeeding'. The sub-groups then share their findings with the whole group and plan methods of overcoming the difficulties listed.

COMMENT

This activity can be used at any time when the group seems to be losing motivation to succeed, or following the activity 'What motivates me?' (see page 74). Some of the issues that come up may need to be added to the group's agreed ground rules.

USE ALSO FOR

Energising, stimulating learning and problem solving.

5 What I want

AIMS

- To motivate group members
- To set personal goals
- To share goals and reasons for being in the group
- To introduce people to each other and break down barriers
- To start building shared interests and trust
- To obtain feedback on how successful participants feel the group has been

PREPARATION *materials needed*

Pens and paper for participants to make notes.

THE ACTIVITY

Invite the group members to pair up with a partner, introduce themselves and share what they would like to take away from this session – for example, a new skill, increased knowledge about something specific, an ability to do something better, new ideas or a feeling of having enjoyed themselves. After a set time, each person tells the whole group their partner's name and what he wants to take away from the group.

VARIATION

Invite each group member to discuss with his partner a goal or ambition and how the group/session will help them to achieve it. After a set time, each person shares their partner's name, his ambition and how he wants the session to contribute to it.

COMMENT

Activities during the session can be adapted to match individual expectations and needs. The activity can be repeated at the end of the session. This time, simply invite each person, in turn, to state whether they feel the group has met their expectations and, if not, why not. Group leaders should leave the group after instructing them to do this activity. A group member can be appointed to write down a summary of the comments, with no names included. This ensures that negative remarks can be made honestly and without fear.

USE ALSO FOR

Building trust and energising.

Affirmations

PREPARATION *materials needed*

Provide a flipchart, magic marker, pens and paper.

THE ACTIVITY

Lead a discussion with the participants about the 'inner voice' that everyone has and the negative things it may say, particularly when we are feeling low. Invite everyone to call out some of the negative things that their voice tells them. List a few of these down one side of the flipchart. Go through each negative statement; opposite it, write a positive affirmation that could replace it. Examples might be as follows:

Negative voice	Positive affirmation
→ I can't do this	→ I have learned from past experience and I can do it
→ You are being silly	→ No, asking questions about things I don't know is how I can learn
→ It isn't worth it	→ I feel proud and happy when I achieve something
→ Nobody cares	→ I care and it means everything to my husband to see me happy

Explain that everyone's positive affirmation will be different, as it will be personal to them. Give out pens and paper and ask each participant to write down five negative things that his inner voice tells him, along with a positive affirmation to replace each one. When they have finished tell them to learn these off by heart and keep the paper with them so that when their inner voice is being negative they can respond with positive affirmations.

VARIATION

Having explained about the negative inner voice, split participants into pairs or small groups. Ask them to share their personal negative inner voice statements and help each other form positive affirmations to replace them. When back in the larger group, volunteers can be asked to share their statements.

COMMENT

Affirmations can be used in all areas of life, including work, personal or social life and when feeling negative about completing a task. Remind group members about their affirmations when they are feeling down or negative.

USE ALSO FOR

Energising and problem solving.

AIMS

↑ To sustain motivation
↑ To maintain a positive attitude
↑ To believe in the ability to succeed

5 Negative to positive

AIMS

AIMS

↑ To raise awareness of what will take away motivation

↑ To explore how to be successful

↑ To think creatively

↑ To share common aims and goals

↑ To build trust between group members

PREPARATION *materials needed*

Provide a flipchart, magic marker, pens and paper.

THE ACTIVITY

Write the group goals on the flipchart. Now ask the group members the question, 'What can we do to make sure that the group fails?' Write a list on the flipchart and then ask 'How can we turn these negatives into positives and ensure that the group succeeds?' Discuss and write the conclusions on the flipchart.

VARIATION

Have group members write down their own personal goals and make a list of what they can do to make sure they fail. This can be completed individually or in pairs. They then write down what they need to do to make sure they succeed, and these conclusions can be shared with the whole group.

COMMENT

Reverse thinking can be a useful strategy when group members run out of ideas or are having difficulty being creative.

USE ALSO FOR

Building trust and managing behaviour and personal responsibility.

Why am I here?

PREPARATION *materials needed*

Provide a flipchart, pens and paper.

THE ACTIVITY

Instruct group members to close their eyes, relax and think about why they are attending. Ask them to think about what they will gain from the group/session/course and to imagine what life will be like when it is finished. Ask them to imagine:

→ what they will be able to do

→ themselves doing it

→ how they will feel.

Allow a few moments and then ask the participants to open their eyes. Give each person paper and pen, and ask them to draw or write about what they imagined.

When everyone has finished, divide participants into pairs and ask them to show, describe and discuss their imagined success. Request that they consider:

→ whether what they imagined is possible

→ what difference it will make if it is true

→ how it will feel.

After a set time, bring the group back together and discuss how the activity has gone. How easy or difficult was it to imagine success? Were they surprised by their imagination?

VARIATION

Divide the group into pairs or sub-groups and have them discuss and list reasons for why the group is important to them. Bring everyone back together and ask them to call out what is on their lists; write the reasons on the flipchart.

COMMENT

This is a good activity for giving new motivation to a flagging group. It also teaches a technique that participants can use themselves when feeling low and lacking in motivation.

USE ALSO FOR

Energising and stimulating learning.

AIMS

↑ To increase motivation

↑ To give each person a personal reason to succeed

↑ To confirm in participants' minds why they are in the group

5 Decisions

AIMS

↑ To motivate group members to achieve personal goals

↑ To show the value of setting criteria

↑ To provide a tool to help when making decisions

PREPARATION *materials needed*

Prepare a problem to be solved or a decision to be made for each sub-group. Provide large sheets of paper and magic markers or pens and paper.

THE ACTIVITY

Split the participants into small groups. Explain that in order to make good decisions, problems need to be analysed. Give each group a problem or decision to be made. For example, it might be that they are going to move to a new area and have to choose a new school for their six year old son. There are several schools to choose from; ask the groups to list the criteria on which a choice is to be made.

After 10 or 15 minutes, invite each sub-group to share its criteria with the whole group and to discuss any problems encountered. Next ask them:

→ Does setting the criteria help motivate you to make the decision?

→ What would happen if you did not set criteria?

→ Does setting criteria help to make the decision easier?

→ What other personal goals, problems or decisions could be helped by setting criteria?

VARIATION

Have each group choose their own decision that is to be made and set the criteria.

COMMENT

People often put off making decisions because they fear that they may make the wrong one. Setting criteria brings clarity and usually breaks down the barrier to making the decision.

USE ALSO FOR

Energising and problem solving.

What is important?

PREPARATION *materials needed*

Provide pens or pencils and paper.

THE ACTIVITY

Provide each group member with a pen and paper and explain to them that in this session they will be drawing their own coat of arms. First, instruct them to draw a shield and to divide it into four sections. Then ask them to draw in each section an item that represents something important to them. This could be:

→ a fortress, to show solidarity

→ two people embracing, to show friendship

→ someone working, to indicate work

→ a pile of money, to indicate wealth

When everyone has completed their coat of arms invite them, in turn, to share their drawing and what it shows.

VARIATION

Adapt the activity to suit the subject of the session. For example, you invite participants to draw four things that are important to them:

→ at work

→ within the family

→ in their social life

→ in the group

COMMENT

It is surprising how often people fail to think about what is important to them. This can then prevent them from being fully aware of actions that contribute to their aspirations.

USE ALSO FOR

Building trust and energising.

AIMS

↑ To clarify what is important

↑ To raise awareness about beliefs

↑ To help develop a sense of self

5 Strength review

AIMS

↑ To improve motivation

↑ To review strengths

↑ To explore ability to make changes

↑ To encourage risk taking

PREPARATION *materials needed*

Provide a flipchart, magic marker, pens and paper.

THE ACTIVITY

Ask the group members to call out some of the changes that people have to make as they travel through life, to describe briefly any changes that they have themselves had to make. For example:

→ changing jobs

→ being married

→ moving from home to single accommodation

→ changing departments at work

→ obtaining a qualification

→ working evening shifts instead of day shifts

→ being unemployed

→ adjusting to being alone after a long time in a steady relationship

Write the changes on a flipchart and then ask participants to choose two changes; explain that they do not have to be thinking of making these changes at present. Hand out two sheets of paper to each person and ask them to write one of their chosen changes at the top of each sheet. On the left-hand side of each sheet they should write the heading 'strengths' and on the right-hand side 'weaknesses'. Now ask them to list four of their own strengths that would help them to deal with the chosen changes, should they have to make them. They can also add up to four weaknesses. When this has been completed, ask them to think about specific ways in which they could counteract the weaknesses.

Finally, examine as a group:

→ what individuals found out about themselves

→ what ideas they gained from listing their weaknesses

→ whether they could apply the same techniques to motivation, to help them to make any desired changes

VARIATION

Complete the exercise in pairs or small groups.

COMMENT

This activity highlights each participant's ability to cope and encourages the group members to believe that what they want to do is possible. Changes can be suggested that fit with the purpose of the group.

USE ALSO FOR

Energising and problem solving.

5 Sharing

AIMS

↑ To remove barriers to motivation

↑ To raise awareness about sharing goals with those giving support

↑ To elicit support and cooperation from family and friends

PREPARATION *materials needed*

A flipchart and magic marker will be useful to note issues and actions. Provide pens and paper so that participants can make notes.

THE ACTIVITY

Ask the group members the following questions; then discuss the reasons why both the questions and the answers are important to them:

→ Have you shared your goals/ambitions with your partner/ family? (If not, why not?)

→ Do you often talk about your goals and progress with them? (If not they may be unaware of how important it is to you.)

→ Do you talk about your goals/ambitions so much that others feel swamped and unimportant?

→ Does your progress mean that others have to make changes too? Do you talk about the effect that this has on them?

→ Do you show your appreciation to and thank those who support you? How?

→ Do you reciprocate by supporting them to achieve what they want?

End by inviting each person to take stock of the issues that have come out of the discussion and consider any action that they can appropriately take.

VARIATION

Brainstorm and discuss with group members any problems that attending the group may generate. Share actions that will ensure that support is maintained and barriers are avoided.

COMMENT

The effect that someone attending a group can have on those around him is often ignored and can become a barrier to motivation that ends with the participant giving up.

USE ALSO FOR

Energising and problem solving.

Values

5

PREPARATION *materials needed*

Provide a flipchart, magic marker, pens and paper.

THE ACTIVITY

Ask the group to call out values that are important to them and write these on the flipchart. The values may include:

→ being respectful
→ being open-minded
→ being independent
→ being truthful
→ supporting my family
→ being loyal
→ being there for my family

AIMS

↑ To raise awareness of conflicts with personal values that demotivate
↑ To examine values that are important to group members
↑ To remove barriers to motivation

When the list is complete, ask each group member to write down five values that are important to them personally. The group now discusses whether there are any inconsistencies between the values they have written down and the goals they are working towards. Are there any conflicts with values held by their partners or other members of their families? How do these affect them and their motivation in the group? How might these conflicts be resolved?

VARIATION

After everyone has written down their values, split participants into sub-groups to discuss conflicts between their goals and values. Finish by bringing the large group together again and ask each sub-group to feed back any conflicts they have identified. Discuss what effect these conflicts may have on motivation.

COMMENT

This activity can reveal conflicts that are not easily resolved. However, acknowledging the conflict is the first step towards resolving it.

USE ALSO FOR

Energising, stimulating learning and problem solving.

5 Boxed in

↑ To motivate group members to make changes

↑ To show how life or a situation can make one feel like being in a box

↑ To demonstrate that people can 'step out of their box' if they are unhappy with it

↑ To explore the positive and negative aspects of how people live

PREPARATION *materials needed*

Obtain a cardboard box for each group member. Alternatively, use masking tape to mark out squares on the floor large enough for one person to stand in. Lay the boxes or squares out in sets of two boxes or squares placed closely together. Provide a flipchart and magic marker.

THE ACTIVITY

Invite each group member to stand in a box or in one of the squares. Ask them to think of a 'box' they feel trapped in. This could be a situation, a relationship, a commitment, a dilemma, a negative attitude, a job, a duty etc., and it may be situated:

→ at work

→ in their personal life

→ in their social life

→ in a relationship

→ in some other area appropriate to the group

Instruct participants to describe the 'box' in which they feel trapped to the person in the box nearest them while remaining in their boxes. Individuals can ask each other for clarification but may not make comments or judgements about each other's boxes. Allow between five and 10 minutes for everyone to explore their situation.

When the time is up, instruct participants to suggest ideas to the person nearby as to how they might be able to step out of the box they have described. After a short period, request that individuals, one at a time, call out suggestions they had to help them step out of their box. Write these on a flipchart.

Now ask the participants to step out of their cardboard boxes and destroy them or pull the masking tape off the floor and put it in the bin. Complete the exercise by discussing reactions and learning from them.

VARIATION

Divide the participants into four sub-groups – or more if a very large group. Using masking tape, draw out four separate 'islands' on the floor – one for each sub-group. Each group stands on their island. Each person imagines they are trapped on their island. Now ask the participants to think of ways in which they feel trapped in their work, personal life, and so on. After a moment or two for thought, invite the sub-group members to share with each other the ways in which they feel trapped.

After five to 10 minutes, invite participants, within their sub-groups, to suggest ways to each other in which they might escape from their private traps. Allow another five to 10 minutes and then ask everyone to share ideas for escaping from their traps. Write the ideas on a flipchart and then instruct participants to destroy their islands and return to their seats. Finish by discussing reactions and learning from them.

COMMENT

A good exercise to encourage people to think creatively about changes they could make. It also helps people to make that creative leap and think 'outside the box'!

USE ALSO FOR

Energising, stimulating learning and problem solving.

5 Challenging questions

AIMS

↑ To motivate participants by involving them

↑ To increase interest by focusing on what participants want to know

↑ To confirm group members' knowledge

↑ To challenge perceptions and provide opportunity for adjustment

PREPARATION *materials needed*

A flipchart, pad and pens.

THE ACTIVITY

Outline the topic that is to be discussed in the activity. Invite the participants to frame as many questions as possible about it – either as one large group or in small sub-groups. If working as a large group, write the group's questions on a flipchart. If working in sub-groups, ask each group to provide you with their questions to be written on the flipchart. Questions can be ranked and dealt with in the ranked order; alternatively, you could invite participants, in turn, to choose questions. Discuss each question as a group.

VARIATION

Have participants work in sub-groups to pose the questions. These are written on the flipchart. The complete list of questions is then divided between the other sub-groups, who discuss their allotted questions and present their conclusions.

COMMENT

This will help you to present a topic in an interesting way and to ensure the involvement of all group members.

USE ALSO FOR

Stimulating learning and assessment and evaluation.

Positive comments

PREPARATION *materials needed*

Provide pens and paper.

THE ACTIVITY

Split the group members into pairs. Ask each participant to imagine himself as a person who knows exactly what to do to make his partner feel good and see the value of what he is achieving through the group. Allow the group members to think for a moment about what they can say to their partner, making notes if they wish.

When everyone is ready, instruct the participants to talk to their partners and say what they have worked out that will boost how the partner feels.

Finish by bringing everyone back together as a large group and discussing how the activity felt. Suggest that the participants can give each other a boost like this at any time: during a break for refreshments, when having a chat after the session, and so on.

VARIATION

Tell the group members to mix at random and make positive statements to each other.

COMMENT

At first, some participants may feel awkward about making such statements and may feel that this activity does not seem genuine. However, positive comments, repeated on a regular basis, really do have an effect.

USE ALSO FOR

Energising and stimulating learning.

AIMS

↑ To motivate group members

↑ To lift the mood of a flagging group

↑ To support each other

↑ To build each person's self-esteem

5 A sense of purpose

PREPARATION *materials needed*

Provide pens and paper.

THE ACTIVITY

1 Explain that most people need a sense of purpose and personal values to guide them to achieve what they want from life. The purposes of the group must be in harmony with participants' personal values.

2 Give out pens and paper and ask each participant to define in a short sentence what he wants from life. This may be to be happy, to have a family, to be a successful writer, to be a good parent, and so on.

3 Now ask everyone to write down a short list of what values are important to them in life. These might be loyalty, respect, honesty, integrity, faith and so on.

4 Invite participants to define what they want from the group in a short sentence. This might be increased confidence, improved parenting skills, better communication, overcoming a fear, and so on.

5 Next, ask participants to examine what they have written. Do the values fit with what they want from life or are they in conflict? Is membership of the group a step towards their goal?

6 Discuss as a group any conflicts. How can conflicts of purpose and values be made consistent?

VARIATION

Have participants work in pairs or small groups to support each other.

COMMENT

This exercise can identify conflicts that hinder motivation. These may have been lingering in the background and participants may not have wanted to acknowledge or deal with them.

USE ALSO FOR

Energising and problem solving.

Problem solving

Exercises and activities to aid problem solving and to help deal with difficulties within the group.

6 Making collective decisions

- ↑ To help group members explore options and reach a collective decision
- ↑ To enable a collective decision to be reached when group members disagree or have different views
- ↑ To encourage group members to take responsibility for decisions

PREPARATION *materials needed*

Provide a chalkboard, whiteboard or flipchart to write on, and chalk or magic markers.

THE ACTIVITY

1   Set a problem, question or challenge and ensure that everyone in the group understands it. The challenge might involve deciding:

   ⇒ what to do

   ⇒ who is going to do something

   ⇒ how to do something

   ⇒ how to resolve something the group members disagree about

   If necessary, get group members to write down on a piece of paper their understanding of the problem, in their own words. Then have them read this out.

   Alternatively, ask them to explain verbally and write the explanations on the flipchart.

2   Have the group members suggest ideas about how to overcome the problem, different viewpoints on the question or what to do to meet the challenge. Write all possibilities on the flipchart or board.

3   The group members now discuss all the solutions, taking them one at a time and examining advantages and disadvantages. Group members may decide at the end of the discussion which is the best solution. If they do not continue to step 4.

4   Eliminate solutions that people agree would not work, would be unacceptable or are unpopular. The group should be left with two, three or no more than four of the most acceptable solutions.

5   Ask the group members to consider what changes need to be made to any of the solutions to make them acceptable. Enquire whether they would be willing to try one of them for a short trial period. If this is not acceptable, go on to step 6.

6   Label the different solutions 1, 2, 3, 4, and so on. Ask each person to choose the three most acceptable solutions. Count up the number of votes for each solution. The solution which has the highest number of votes becomes the accepted solution.

VARIATION

It is not always necessary to use the whole procedure. Steps 1 to 3 frequently produce a solution. You may wish to leave out steps 4 and 5 and go straight to step 6 instead. Use whatever elements of the procedure match the group's needs.

COMMENT

Avoid going for a straight vote, show of hands or secret ballot, as these methods produce 'winners' and 'losers'. The above procedure avoids the group members being 'split' over a decision. Use it when participants are struggling to agree.

USE ALSO FOR

Managing behaviour and personal responsibility.

6 Who listens?

AIMS

↑ To encourage group members to improve their listening skills

↑ To demonstrate the importance of listening

↑ To show how communication may falter and misunderstanding may occur

PREPARATION *materials needed*

Provide pens and paper. A flipchart and magic marker will also be useful to make lists.

THE ACTIVITY

Explain the purpose of the exercise (improving listening skills) and give out pens and paper. Instruct the participants to write down three ways in which communication could be improved within the group. When this has been completed, ask each group member to choose a partner. The members of each pair decide between them who is going to be 'A' and who 'B'.

Next invite all the 'A's to read their first idea out to the 'B's, and the 'B's to comment on the idea. Allow a set time for this and then ask the 'B's to read out their first idea to the 'A's and the 'A's to comment. This continues until all the ideas have been read out and commented on.

Bring everyone back together as a large group and request everyone writes down all the ideas their partner had and what comments they had about their own ideas. After a set time ask them how well they did in recalling each others' ideas and comments. What difficulties did they encounter?

→ Was anyone thinking about other things while their partner was talking? What were they thinking?

→ Was anyone judging their partner's ideas and comments rather than listening and trying to understand?

→ Was anyone rehearsing their reactions to ideas or comments instead of listening?

→ Was anyone worrying or concentrating on what they were going to say rather than listening?

End by discussing how understanding and communication are affected by poor listening skills and explore some methods for improving them.

VARIATION

Use other topics to stimulate ideas that are relevant to the group. For example:

→ three ways to improve your parenting skills

→ three ways to be more assertive

The number of ideas could also be increased to make the exercise more difficult.

COMMENT

Use this activity when problems arise from group members not listening to each other. How much more people would learn and understand if only they listened and understood each other.

USE ALSO FOR

Building trust and managing behaviour and personal responsibility.

6 Solving problems

AIMS

↑ To demonstrate the value of working together

↑ To encourage everyone to contribute

↑ To practise a proven method for solving problems

PREPARATION *materials needed*

Think of a problem for the group to solve or ask the group to propose a problem that one of them would like to solve. Provide a flipchart, magic marker and pens and paper.

THE ACTIVITY

Write the problem on the flipchart. Give out pens and paper to each participant and instruct them to work alone and write down as many ideas as they can for solving the problem. When this has been completed invite everyone to call out their ideas and write them on the flipchart. Watch the list of ideas expand.

When all the ideas have been written on the flipchart, ask each participant to count the number of ideas that had not occurred to him. End by having participants suggest what other opportunities there may be to find solutions to problems by talking and working with other people and sharing ideas. This should include all aspects of life, such as relationships, work, the group, and social and family life.

VARIATION

After everyone has written down their own ideas for solving the problem, invite them to form small groups to share and add to their ideas. After a set time bring everyone together again as a large group to discuss the advantages of working together.

COMMENT

This is a useful exercise to use when group members are not working well together or are failing to support each other. It helps them to share knowledge and experience.

USE ALSO FOR

Motivation and managing behaviour and personal responsibility.

How do you feel?

PREPARATION *materials needed*

Provide a flipchart, magic marker, pens and paper.

THE ACTIVITY

Involve the group members in a quick brainstorm of words that describe feelings, and write them on the flipchart. Ensure that both negative and positive feelings are included. Your list might include:

- → aggressive
- → anxious
- → arrogant
- → resentful
- → surprised
- → hurt

- → hungry
- → indifferent
- → jealous
- → cold
- → confident
- → horrified

- → disappointed
- → curious
- → bored
- → enraged
- → angry
- → frustrated

- → tearful
- → interested
- → frightened
- → envious
- → guilty
- → worried

AIMS

- ↑ To reveal feelings at the beginning and end of sessions
- ↑ To deal with feelings that might be a barrier at the beginning of the session
- ↑ To help group members start to share feelings and build trust
- ↑ To deal with feelings at the end of sessions

When a the list is complete, give each participant a pen and paper. Ask each person to write down the word on the list that best describes how he is feeling. Now invite each participant, in turn, to state their word – giving an opportunity for them to expand on it if they wish. If they are willing, try to elicit why they are feeling as they do (but don't force it). This provides an opportunity to address issues related to the group. Ask everyone to keep their slip until the end of the session.

At the end of the session, ask the participants to refer back to their initial feeling word and write down what they now feel. Again, invite everyone to share and deal with what is revealed. For many, negative feelings at the beginning of the session will have shifted to being more positive. If more negative feelings are revealed, it may be necessary to look at the content of the session.

VARIATION

Go around the room asking participants how they feel; do this again at the end of the session. It is worth noting the words people use at the start, to compare with what they say at the end.

COMMENT

It is sometimes useful to have a quick 'feeling check' in the middle of the session, and this can help people feel supported. It is important when doing this exercise that you help people to feel comfortable about revealing negative feelings.

USE ALSO FOR

Building trust, motivation and managing behaviour and personal responsibility.

6 Putting concerns to one side

AIMS

↑ To enable group members to relax

↑ To ensure that worries and concerns about matters outside the group do not interfere with the session

↑ To help participants focus on the activities

PREPARATION *materials needed*

Provide a box, envelopes, paper and pens.

THE ACTIVITY

Hand out an envelope, paper and pen to each participant. Invite each participant to write a list of concerns that were on his mind prior to the session. This might be: deciding what to cook for dinner, arranging an important appointment, buying a birthday present, preparing for an interview, and so on. Reassure everyone that no-one is going to see what they write. When the lists are complete, ask everyone to put their list in the envelope provided, seal it and write their name on it. Now collect the envelopes, put them in a box – emphatically closing the lid – and inform participants that you are putting them away, out of sight and out of mind, and that you want them to do the same. Say you will keep them safe and will give them back their problems at the end of the session. When the session ends, bring the box out and hand back each participant's list of worries.

VARIATION

Instead of collecting the envelopes in a box, tell everyone to put their envelopes away somewhere safe and out of sight such as in a handbag or a jacket pocket. Have them take them out again at the end of the session.

COMMENT

A simple exercise that is surprisingly effective. Somehow, having written the worry on the list and put it out of sight, people are more able to put the worry to one side for a time. This enables them to focus better.

USE ALSO FOR

Building trust, motivation and managing behaviour and personal responsibility.

Confidence boost

PREPARATION *materials needed*

None.

THE ACTIVITY

Ask each participant, in turn, to state something they do well. Examples might be:

→ I am a good cook

→ I am good at football

→ I am a good friend

→ I am good at cheering other people up

→ I am good at embroidery

Go round the group two or three times, so everyone identifies a number of things they are good at.

VARIATION

Instead, have a few rounds of participants telling the group something that they enjoy doing.

COMMENT

Use this activity when the group needs cheering up, is feeling low or is finding things difficult.

USE ALSO FOR

Energising and managing behaviour and personal responsibility.

AIMS

↑ To give group members a confidence boost

↑ To change the mood of the group

↑ To engender a positive attitude

6 Mind clearance

AIMS

↑ To help participants clear their minds at the beginning of a session

↑ To enable everyone to focus on the topic

↑ To offload thoughts and issues that could interfere with concentration

PREPARATION *materials needed*

None

THE ACTIVITY

Ask each person, in turn, to state how their week or day has gone so far, briefly describing anything significant that has happened to them (such as having a night out, achieving something, solving a problem, and so on). Each participant should take only one or two minutes and then the next person recalls their events during the past week.

VARIATION

Invite everyone to state something good or enjoyable that has happened to them since the last group meeting. These can be small things, such as enjoying a meal, some music, a walk, a conversation, and so on.

COMMENT

People often rush to groups with their minds full of thoughts about what has just happened. Sharing recent events provides a safety valve, enabling participants to settle down. It also makes them feel acknowledged, what happens to them is important, that they matter.

USE ALSO FOR

Introductions and icebreakers, energising, motivation and managing behaviour and personal responsibility.

Problems and solutions

PREPARATION *materials needed*

Provide a flipchart, magic marker, pens and chart handouts.

THE ACTIVITY

Invite the group members to contribute problems they have encountered, or use those listed in the left-hand column of the table below. Write them on the flipchart using a table as shown. Next, discuss what the cause of the problem is in each case and write this on the flipchart. Finally, discuss alternative, more satisfactory, solutions to the problem and add these to the table.

AIMS

↑ To demonstrate a method of thinking about problems in a different way

↑ To avoid looking at a problem in the same old way

↑ To examine the root cause of problems

PROBLEM	CAUSE OF PROBLEM	ALTERNATIVE SOLUTION
Eating too much	Wanting comfort when stressed	
Always being late	Wanting to be the centre of attention	
Talking too much	Being nervous/tense	
Abrupt manner	Shyness or not knowing what to say	

Talk through the various possible solutions to each problem: suitable solutions will vary from person to person.

VARIATION

Sheets showing the above chart can be handed out for participants to work on individually or with a partner.

COMMENT

This is a useful way of working through problems within the group as well as those that individuals may experience. Once you have demonstrated the technique, blank charts can be given out so that participants may use them to work on their own problems.

USE ALSO FOR

Motivation, managing behaviour and personal responsibility.

One at a time

6

PREPARATION *materials needed*

Have a ball ready to use.

THE ACTIVITY

Arrange everyone in a circle. Hold the ball and explain that any participant who wants to speak must hold it while they do so. No-one can speak until they have possession of it. When they have finished speaking, they place the ball in the centre, so anyone else who wants to speak can pick it up. Alternatively, the ball can be handed to anyone who has indicated they would like to speak next. Introduce the topic that you want the group to discuss and place the ball in the centre, or hand it to the participant who wants to speak first. The activity continues in this way until the allotted time is up.

VARIATION

Put a limit on how long anyone can keep the ball before handing it on to someone else.

COMMENT

This is a very useful strategy to use when discussing controversial or heated topics. The procedure is also very effective in preventing any one person from dominating a discussion.

USE ALSO FOR

Managing behaviour and personal responsibility.

AIMS

↑ To ensure that all participants have an opportunity to speak

↑ To avoid anyone dominating the discussion

6 Stressed out

PREPARATION *materials needed*

Provide a flipchart and magic marker.

THE ACTIVITY

Begin by discussing with the group members what the sources of stress in the group might be; write these on the flipchart. The stresses identified might include: having to get to the group on time, not having completed tasks set last session, not being able to keep up, being under pressure to give up, having to contribute in the sessions, and so on. Next, discuss techniques for dealing with the problems identified. End by asking each group member to identify something that has been discussed that they could use to deal with any stress they are experiencing now or could experience in the future.

VARIATION

After identifying possible sources of stress, write these on a flipchart, asking each person to identify and write down something in the group that is causing them stress or might do in the future. Ask each person to choose a partner to work with, discussing solutions to each of their identified stressors. After a set time, bring everyone back together as a group and share their solutions.

COMMENT

Use this activity at the beginning of a session, or later if stress becomes evident.

USE ALSO FOR

Building trust and energising.

There is always a bright side

PREPARATION *materials needed*

Provide a flipchart and magic marker.

THE ACTIVITY

Explain that everyone is going to have opportunity to consider something negative and explore positive outcomes. Ask each person to complete the sentence 'I hate it when ......' For example, one person might state 'I hate it when *it rains*'. Give each person in the group the opportunity to make a statement and write them all on the flipchart. Then take each statement one at a time and have everyone call out what might be positive outcomes from it. For example, the statement 'I hate it when it rains' might generate positive outcome comments such as 'It's good for the garden', 'It will help avoid water shortages', 'The air feels fresher after a shower', and so on. Go through all the statements in this way, collating as many positive outcomes as possible.

VARIATION

Form small sub-groups and have each one complete the process for every member.

COMMENT

Use this exercise when you want everyone to take a positive view of what is going to be introduced next or when group members are feeling negative.

USE ALSO FOR

Energising and motivation.

AIMS

↑ To prepare to introduce a topic on a positive note

↑ To lift the mood of the group

↑ To learn a technique that challenges negative thinking

6 Making assumptions

AIMS

↑ To make people aware of the assumptions they may be making

↑ To help build trust

↑ To raise awareness of prejudice

↑ To encourage participants to investigate facts rather than jump to conclusions

PREPARATION *materials needed*

Provide six suitably numbered pictures or written descriptions of people interacting. Also provide pens and paper.

THE ACTIVITY

Give each person a pencil and paper. Instruct them to write the numbers one to six down one side of the paper. Tell participants that you are going to pass around some numbered pictures. When a picture is passed to them they write alongside the number what they think is happening in the picture. Participants must not talk to each other or exchange ideas. When everyone has completed the task, show the pictures one at a time and ask group members what they have written for each one.

Discuss the interpretations given and examine any assumptions made. What evidence is there for some of the interpretations? Which have been based on facts?

Point out that everyone makes assumptions. Can group members think of incidents in their own lives when they have made assumptions about people? What assumptions have people in the group made about each other? Might some of these assumptions be wrong?

VARIATION

Use written descriptions of incidents rather than pictures.

COMMENT

Use this exercise when group members have been making assumptions or exhibiting prejudice about each other. For example, they may have made assumptions which relate to the cultural or religious backgrounds, sexual orientation or age of a fellow group member, and they may have stereotyped the person.

USE ALSO FOR

Building trust and managing behaviour and personal responsibility.

Negotiating solutions

6

PREPARATION *materials needed*

Have available flipchart sheets and magic markers.

THE ACTIVITY

Split the participants into two groups. Name one group 'red' and the other 'blue'. Explain that the blue group wants to provide affordable housing on a local open field that was formerly a 'green' site. Young people and industries are leaving the area because they cannot get housing, the area is becoming run down and unemployment is high. The red group strongly opposes the idea of building on the green area, on environmental grounds.

Give each team a flipchart sheet and a magic marker and ask them to write down words or phrases that express how they might view the people in the other team, who oppose what they want.

When the task has been completed, bring the groups together to share what has been written. Display the two flipchart sheets and ask the participants to identify and cross out any stereotypes. Next, have them call out characteristics, values, attitudes or beliefs that both teams might have in common and write these on another flipchart sheet alongside the other two.

Finally, facilitate a discussion about what has been discovered from this activity. Ask the group the following questions:

→ Do those of you who were in opposing groups feel very different from each other?

→ Should stereotyping be avoided? Why?

→ How can common characteristics be used to help communication between two opposing parties?

→ What have you learned that might help negotiations between two groups?

→ Would it be possible for the two parties to negotiate as *partners* rather than as *opponents*?

→ How can you use this process to solve problems you encounter, and avoid seeing as opponents those who disagree with you?

→ Can you cite past incidences when viewing a situation in this way would have been helpful?

AIMS

↑ To identify common ground

↑ To encourage open communication

↑ To identify barriers to agreement

↑ To promote diversity

VARIATION

Use a different problem within the group – one that relates to the group sessions, perhaps.

COMMENT

This is another activity that can be used to promote diversity in relation to stereotyping of cultural, gender or different backgrounds.

USE ALSO FOR

Building trust and managing behaviour and personal responsibilities.

Cooperation

PREPARATION *materials needed*

Find a variety of different pictures, from magazines or posters, for example – one for each group member. Cut each picture into three pieces. Put three pieces from different pictures in envelopes – one envelope for each group member.

THE ACTIVITY

Give each group member an envelope. The task is for each person, by negotiating non-verbally with others, to complete a picture. Participants must not speak during the activity. When it has been completed, discuss as a group:

→ How important, and how difficult was communication?

→ What methods did you use to assist communication?

→ How did you feel during the exercise?

→ Were there any misunderstandings?

→ Did some people block others from completing their pictures? What were the consequences of this?

→ Did some of you help each other?

→ Would the task have been completed more quickly and easily if everyone had cooperated?

VARIATION

Instead of pictures, use sheets of newspaper or magazine pages for the exercise.

COMMENT

The exercise can be made more difficult by cutting the picture or newspaper sheet into four or five pieces.

USE ALSO FOR

Stimulating learning and managing behaviour and personal responsibility.

AIMS

↑ To explore non-verbal communication

↑ To encourage group members to work in a cooperative way

↑ To raise awareness of difficulties with communication

↑ To emphasise the importance of communication and problem solving in gaining cooperation

6 Guided fantasy

AIMS

AIMS

↑ To prepare group members for the session

↑ To reduce stress or anxiety

↑ To enable group members to focus on the session

↑ To help people relax

PREPARATION *materials needed*

None, though you might like some soft relaxing music to play in the background.

THE ACTIVITY

Seat participants in comfortable chairs. Tell everyone to lean back, rest their head on the back of the chair, their arms on the arms of the chair and close their eyes. Say, 'Take a deep breath and let it out slowly. Feel tension drain away, down your body and legs, through your feet and into the ground. Now concentrate on something that you find relaxing, this might be a mental picture of a stream, a piece of music, a pleasant smell or a sound. Let anything that is worrying you fade from your mind. Don't try to force it away, let it drift in and out and float away. Concentrate for a moment on whatever you find relaxing and hold it.'

Allow a moment for people to relax, and then continue: 'Now, gradually imagine yourself coming back to the room. You feel more relaxed, refreshed and ready to enjoy and focus on what we are going to do. Gradually open your eyes, sit up and orientate yourself in the room once again.'

VARIATION

Instead of using something that the participants find relaxing, ask them to imagine themselves concentrating on the session and taking another step towards achieving their goals or ambitions. Lead them through what they are going to do in the session.

COMMENT

This activity can be used at the beginning of a session, or at any time when you sense tension or a lack of concentration. It helps participants to relax, and to concentrate. With slight word alteration, it can also be used at the end of the session to send people on their way feeling good. This is especially useful if the session has been tough.

USE ALSO FOR

Introductions and icebreakers and stimulating learning.

Managing behaviour and personal responsibility

7

Exercises and activities to maintain discipline and collaboration and encourage personal responsibility.

Shared feelings

AIMS

↑ To obtain feedback from the group members when you sense there is a problem, difficulty or issue of concern within the group

↑ To encourage group members to take responsibility for expressing their views and exploring difficulties

PREPARATION *materials needed*

None, but a little forethought and care needs to be taken in how you phrase your statements to encourage a response.

THE ACTIVITY

Stop the group at an appropriate point in the activity and ask for comments. It is important that you remain non-judgemental. State that you sense that something is worrying the group or that there is an issue that has not been fully discussed. You could say something like; 'I don't feel happy with the last activity. It did not seem to go very well. What do you feel about it?' or, 'I sense that some of you feel uncomfortable about what we are doing. Can you stop for a moment and tell me how you feel?'

You will need to respond to comments and suggestions made by the group members and decide whether changes need to be made to the programme, or whether action needs to be taken to deal with issues raised.

VARIATION

Another variation on the above would be: 'I sense that some of you are finding the task too difficult at this stage. How do you feel about it?'

The wording can be changed to fit almost all situations.

COMMENT

It may not be appropriate to hold a lengthy discussion in the middle of an activity but, having identified the problem, discussion time can be scheduled into the programme as necessary. Encourage group members to contribute their views – to raise any difficulties and have them addressed quickly. This helps to give participants a feeling of control over what they are doing and encourages them to take responsibility for their learning. This strategy can be used at any time.

USE ALSO FOR

Problem solving and assessment and evaluation.

Helps and hinders

PREPARATION *materials needed*

Provide pens and paper for volunteer observers. A video or DVD recorder and player will also be needed for the variation.

THE ACTIVITY

Ask for two (or more) volunteers to act as observers during the session. Instruct the observers to list everything they see and hear that helps the group to work well and all the things that hinders or makes progress difficult. Names must not be mentioned, only the behaviours observed. These might include:

Hinders	Helps
→ Interrupting	→ Giving feedback
→ Not contributing	→ Sharing ideas
→ Talking when they should be listening	→ Asking questions
→ Shouting others down	→ Paying compliments

AIMS

↑ To give responsibility for behaviour and progress to participants

↑ To raise awareness of group behaviour and its effects

↑ To help group members examine their behaviour

↑ To enable reflection on what is helpful and what is unhelpful

Towards the end of the session, in a specially allocated time, have the observers give feedback and discuss the issues raised. Only behaviour should be discussed, not who did what.

End the discussion by asking each participant to state what they could do to improve their performance in the group.

VARIATION

Use a video or DVD recorder to record the session or part of it. Replay the recording and have group members observe their own behaviour. After watching the recording, invite the group to discuss what helped and what hindered.

Before videoing any group, make sure that everyone agrees to the procedure and that they know what will happen to the recording afterwards; it is usually best to erase or destroy it. A drawback of videoing is that participants may be very conscious of the camera.

COMMENT

As part of this exercise it may be necessary to revisit any group ground rules that have previously been agreed and amend them as appropriate.

USE ALSO FOR

Stimulating learning and problem solving.

Feel good

AIMS

↑ To encourage participants to take responsibility for their own behaviour and the effect it has on others

↑ To have the group members reflect on the effects of 'put downs'

↑ To boost people's self-esteem

PREPARATION *materials needed*

Paper, pens, a flipchart and magic markers.

THE ACTIVITY

Ask each participant to write down on a piece of paper a 'put down' that they have experienced. It may be something that someone else has said or something that they tell themselves. Examples are:

→ Anyone could have done that

→ My brother is good at that

→ I'm hopeless at everything

→ She's just a housewife

→ What do you expect? He's disabled

→ You're useless at that

→ You're stupid!

Collect the pieces of paper and shuffle them. Read the 'put downs' out and write them on the flipchart. Discuss how the participants feel when they are spoken about in this way. What effect do such comments have? How should they be dealt with? There is no need for anyone to identify their statements unless they feel comfortable doing so.

After discussion, move on to what makes group members feel good. Do this by having each group member complete the statement 'I feel good when …' Responses might be: 'I feel good when…:

→ … someone pays me a compliment

→ … tells me I have done well

→ … someone says 'thank you' for something I have done for them

→ … we share ideas in the group

A list of positive statements can be made on the flipchart. This can be displayed as reminder for the rest of the session and in future sessions.

VARIATIONS

Instead of having participants write the 'put downs', ask them to call them out and write them on the flipchart. Then discuss the effect they have.

COMMENT

Writing the 'put downs' on paper and keeping them anonymous makes it easier for some people to share statements that they feel sensitive about. Groups may wish to consider whether they want to add something about 'put downs' to the group rules.

USE ALSO FOR

Energising, stimulating learning and problem solving.

Taking responsibility

AIMS

↑ To help group members to examine their behaviour

↑ To enable people to reflect on what is helping and what is hindering progress

↑ To enable individuals to 'own' their own behaviour and to take responsibility for both their own and the group's progress

PREPARATION *materials needed*

Have available pens, a flipchart and magic markers. Prepare a handout with the statements below listed – leaving enough space for personal responses to be written.

→ What I did that helped the group

→ What I did that hindered the group

→ What others did that was helpful

→ What others did that hindered me

THE ACTIVITY

Distribute the handout. Ask group members to reflect on the session or sessions that have been difficult and respond to the statements. Make it clear that no names should be mentioned and no accusations made.

When everyone has had time to reflect and write down responses, go round the group members, one at a time, and have them read their responses aloud. Make notes on the flipchart of the main issues; when everyone has completed their statements, facilitate a discussion. Consider whether the group needs to complete some group rules for behaviour or whether existing group rules need to be changed.

VARIATION

After the discussion, ask participants to make a note of any personal changes that they plan to make and invite them to share these with the group. Changes might be:

→ I will not interrupt other people

→ I will wait my turn

→ I will give feedback to others

→ I will arrive on time

Write the suggested changes on the flipchart and put them on display as a reminder for the remainder of the session and/or the next session.

COMMENT

Make it clear to group members that their personal success and that of the group is their responsibility.

USE ALSO FOR

Building trust, energising and stimulating learning.

Personal priorities

PREPARATION *materials needed*

Have available a flipchart, pens and paper.

THE ACTIVITY

Form small sub-groups of three or four people. Each sub-group discusses why they have joined and what they want to learn from the group. The groups also decide on an agenda from the session or course outline: ask each sub-group to prioritise three items.

Bring everyone back together and list on the flipchart the three items from each group. You may be able to give priority to all the items listed in the session or series of sessions, but it is useful to discuss the items and ask them to prioritise them again so that you have about six items in total – these will be given priority.

VARIATION

Ask each person to arrive for the session with three chosen priorities that they would like to be addressed. List and discuss the chosen items as a group and select six items to prioritise.

COMMENT

Ensure that you stick to the priorities set by the group and that all the items selected are covered as planned.

USE ALSO FOR

Building trust, stimulating learning and motivation.

AIMS

↑ To encourage participants to take personal responsibility
↑ To encourage working together as a group
↑ To give opportunity for participants to set their priorities

Whose habits?

AIMS

↑ To encourage management of one's own habits

↑ To make group members aware of how others see them

↑ To enable individuals to choose to change their habits

PREPARATION *materials needed*

Have slips of paper prepared with a participant's name on each slip. Place in a hat or a bag. Have a game or activity in mind for the participants to take part in.

THE ACTIVITY

Ask the group members to draw a slip of paper from the hat. They must keep the name on the piece of paper to themselves. Instruct everyone to act out their perceptions of the person named while taking part in the next activity. Make it clear that no-one can be destructive but must enter into the planned activity with a sense of fun, in the manner of the person named on their slip of paper. If the person has a habit of speaking slowly they might speak slowly. If the person has a particular mannerism such as rubbing their face, they might emphasise that. No-one is allowed to reveal who they are pretending to be until after the activity or game is completed.

When the game is finished, see if people have recognised themselves and discuss:

➡ how it felt

➡ what can be done about undesirable habits

VARIATION

Discuss habits that people have and give out the names of famous people for participants to mimic. This can then be followed with a discussion on changing undesirable habits.

COMMENT

This activity risks participants feeling some embarrassment. However, as long as trust and confidence in each other has been established, no-one is mocked and the activity is entered into with a sense of fun, it can be effective in enabling participants to realise they can choose to make changes and take responsibility for how they appear to others. The variation is the least challenging for participants.

USE ALSO FOR

Motivation and problem solving.

Working menu

PREPARATION *materials needed*

Have available a flipchart and magic markers.

THE ACTIVITY

Inform the group that you want them to agree a 'working menu'. It is up to them to agree the menu. Ask participants to suggest things that they think will help everyone work together successfully. These might include, for example:

→ listening to each other's point of view

→ respecting confidentiality

→ supporting each other

Write the suggestions on the flipchart. When a list has been agreed, ask participants to reduce it to five or six of the most important ideas. The group then uses these as a guide for good working relationships during the life of the group.

VARIATION

Form several small groups. Each group puts together a working menu. These are then shared in the large group and five or six of the most important ideas are agreed.

COMMENT

This exercise is useful when the group is not cohesive or when participants are not working well together.

USE ALSO FOR

Building trust, stimulating learning, motivation and problem solving.

AIMS

↑ To encourage group members to take responsibility for themselves and for what happens in the group

↑ To build a safe environment in which people feel comfortable

↑ To enable everyone to work together

↑ To build trust

7 Quick on the draw

AIMS

↑ To encourage participants to acknowledge and take responsibility for their feelings

↑ To provide an alternative way of expressing feelings or ambitions

↑ To help individuals build self-awareness

↑ To elicit information about difficult topics

PREPARATION *materials needed*

Provide drawing paper, crayons and pencils.

THE ACTIVITY

Distribute the drawing materials and ask participants to draw two pictures. One should represent how they are feeling in the group now; the other should represent how they would like to feel in the group. The pictures can be diagrammatic, abstract, or of a scene that demonstrates their feelings. Emphasise that they do not have to be well-drawn pictures.

Ask everyone, in turn, to show their pictures and interpret them for the group. Questions can be asked when individuals are explaining their pictures, to enable the feeling drawn to be better understood.

When each person has expressed their feelings any issues that emerge will then need to be addressed.

VARIATION

This procedure can be used widely; for example, you might ask the participants to draw:

→ relationships within a family

→ relationships at work

→ how they see themselves now and how they would like to be in a year or five years' time

→ a family shield with divisions to show different aspects of themselves

COMMENT

This exercise enables the group participants to express how good they feel about the group, as well as being a tool for use when things may be going wrong.

USE ALSO FOR

Motivation and problem solving.

The journey

PREPARATION *materials needed*

Provide flipchart paper and crayons or magic markers.

THE ACTIVITY

Split the group into sub-groups. Give each sub-group a flipchart sheet and magic markers or crayons. Tell the groups that you want them to imagine that they are going on a journey in a minibus which symbolises the group; they are to draw the route the minibus will take to get to its destination. Ask them to draw in any obstacles that the group is likely to encounter and must overcome, for example:

→ bad attitudes

→ not supporting each other

→ partner against them attending the group

→ lack of support at home

→ being negative

→ not cooperating

→ not completing tasks

→ not making an effort

When each sub-group has completed the task, invite them to share their findings with the larger group and discuss how any obstacles might be overcome.

VARIATION

Ask group members to plot their own personal routes to achieve their goals. These are then shared with the group, along with ideas on how obstacles might be overcome.

COMMENT

This activity is useful for identifying blocks that might demotivate participants.

USE ALSO FOR

Motivation and problem solving.

AIMS
↑ To encourage participants to take personal responsibility for the success of the group
↑ To raise awareness of obstacles to the group's success
↑ To support participants in overcoming obstacles

7 Wreckage

AIMS

↑ To encourage group members to take responsibility for their own behaviour

↑ To enable everyone to reflect on what is helpful and what is unhelpful

↑ To provide an opportunity for individuals to own up to their behaviour and make changes

PREPARATION *materials needed*

Have available a flipchart and magic markers.

THE ACTIVITY

Ask the group members to call out the sorts of things that could destroy or spoil the group. These might include: dishonesty, forming cliques, talking about others behind their backs, disclosing confidential information outside the group, and so on. Write a list on the flipchart.

When this has been sufficiently explored, start another list – of behaviours that would help group members to meet their goals.

Having completed both lists, ask participants to reflect briefly on whether any of the behaviours described, either negative or positive, match how they might or do behave themselves. If their behaviour has a negative effect, how might they change it to help both themselves and others to achieve? Pause for reflection, then emphasise the importance of everyone taking responsibility for their own behaviour to ensure the success of the group.

VARIATION

Split the group in two. One sub-group produces a list of behaviours that will wreck the group and the other a list of behaviours that will help the group succeed. The two groups then share their lists and everyone reflects on their own behaviour.

COMMENT

This activity can be used in the first session – or later on if destructive behaviour becomes evident. If used in the first session, continue a stage further and have the group members decide on what group guidelines they would like everyone to abide by. If used in a later session, revisit existing guidelines and make changes as appropriate.

USE ALSO FOR

Motivation and problem solving.

Anonymous notes

PREPARATION *materials needed*

Provide two shades of coloured paper for participants to write on; give each person one sheet of each colour. Also provide a flipchart and magic markers.

THE ACTIVITY

Ask participants to write down two things that make them feel *uncomfortable* in the group; everyone should use the same colour paper for this. On the other coloured piece of paper, ask them to write two things that they *like* about the group.

When everyone has finished writing collect the pieces of paper, keeping the colours separate. Shuffle each pile and then read aloud from papers that state what makes people feel uncomfortable. After reading each one, discuss what the group could do to make that person feel more comfortable. Note on the flipchart any changes in group behaviour or actions required. When all the concerns have been addressed, display the list of actions as a reminder.

Finish by going through all the statements of what people liked about the group.

VARIATION

The statements requested can be changed to suit the group situation. For example, you might ask for:

⇒ Two things I would change in the group

⇒ Two things that would make me feel better about the group

⇒ Two things that have upset me about the group

⇒ Two things that have been disappointing about the group

Whatever statements you ask group members to make, always ensure that you finish on things that they like about the group.

COMMENT

Adapt this activity as necessary and use it when you sense something is wrong but are unable to put your finger on the problem, or when you want to raise group members' awareness about feeling, behaviour or other issues. It can also be used to get feedback on how group members feel the group is progressing.

USE ALSO FOR

Motivation, problem solving and assessment and evaluation.

AIMS

↑ To encourage people to own responsibility for what happens in the group

↑ To support individuals in revealing and discussing difficult or sensitive issues

↑ To promote awareness of behaviour

↑ To provide opportunity for changes in behaviour

7 Viewpoint

AIMS

- To encourage group members to take responsibility for decisions
- To enable everyone to express their viewpoint
- To encourage participation
- To assess support for a suggestion
- To evaluate what has been understood

PREPARATION *materials needed*

Ensure that some chalk or tape is available, and a flipchart and magic markers.

THE ACTIVITY

Draw a chalk line or lay tape in a straight line on the floor. Write a statement on a flipchart sheet and put it at one end of the line. Place an opposing statement at the other end. These could be opinions, choices or suggestions, for example: 'It is OK to tell lies' and 'It is never OK to tell lies', or 'The group should meet twice a week' and 'The group should meet once each week'. Now ask for a volunteer to choose a position along the line that represents their view, and to make a short statement as to why they have chosen that position. Each group member, in turn, does the same. If anyone is reluctant to join in, make a rule that statements do not have to be made and they can simply point to a place on the line if they prefer.

VARIATION

If there are more than two response options a cross or a circle can be made on the floor, with the options placed at different points.

COMMENT

The activity adds a sense of fun to making choices and enables those reluctant to comment to have their views taken into account.

USE ALSO FOR

Energising, problem solving and assessment and evaluation.

Reversal

PREPARATION *materials needed*

Ensure that a flipchart is available, and some magic markers.

THE ACTIVITY

Invite the group members to suggest what behaviours would ensure that the session or sessions would fail, for example: not talking to each other, not paying attention, interrupting, everyone talking at the same time, not cooperating and so on. Compile a list on the flipchart. When the group's ideas are exhausted, ask participants to convert these into positive ground rules that will make the group successful. For example: one participant speaks at a time, everyone encourages others to participate, all group members arrive on time, and so on. Once agreed, the ground rules can be displayed at each session.

AIMS

↑ To encourage personal responsibility
↑ To motivate individuals
↑ To facilitate creative thinking
↑ To agree on guidelines for the group

VARIATION

Invite the participants to write down three things that would ensure that the group fails. These are then shared with the whole group, written on the flipchart and ground rules agreed.

COMMENT

It can be very useful to do this activity at the end of a session or series of sessions. Reinforce what participants can do to transfer what they have learnt in the group to everyday life by asking group members to call out what they can do to ensure that they *fail* in their goals. These suggestions can then be turned into positive actions. This reversal technique is useful when people are having difficulty in thinking creatively.

USE ALSO FOR

Stimulating learning, motivation, problem solving and closures.

 **Obstacles to success**

AIMS

↑ To empower participants to make changes and take personal responsibility for their actions

↑ To raise awareness of what is getting in the way of progress

↑ To encourage people to let go of old influences

PREPARATION *materials needed*

Provide pencils and paper.

THE ACTIVITY

Invite participants to relax and think about anything that comes to mind that prevents them from succeeding in something. It may be the voice of a parent or a friend, other influences from family, workmates or friends, or pictures that are seen in the mind. It may involve beliefs or values. Instruct everyone to write down phrases or thoughts that come to mind.

Then have participants break into small groups to share with each other what they have discovered that they could let go. After a set time, bring everyone back together and have the sub-groups share further.

VARIATION

Continue with a discussion about all the things that other people put in the participants' way that can be got rid of now, rather than waiting for someone else to 'give permission' to let go. Each person has the ability to change many things in their personal attitudes towards succeeding in the group, in their social life, at work or in personal relationships.

COMMENT

This is a useful exercise when personal barriers seem to be holding group members back or when they have become stuck and do not understand why.

USE ALSO FOR

Motivation and problem solving.

Building sensitivity

PREPARATION *materials needed*

Provide a small card for each group member, paper and a pen.

THE ACTIVITY

Hand out the cards and pens, one to each group member. Instruct participants to write something about their past or something that they want to do in the future that no-one in the group could possibly know. Examples might be: 'When I was eight I got lost in the desert', 'I want to write a novel', 'I went to school with David Beckham', 'I haven't spoken to my brother for 10 years', and so on. When everyone has finished writing, collect the cards and shuffle them.

Read aloud what is written on one of the cards and ask group members to write down who they think has written it. Continue through the cards in this manner then go back to the beginning again and see how many people correctly matched the cards to writer. As you go through each one, ask what clues participants used to match people to their statements. Allow anyone who wants to expand on their written statement to do so.

Finally, discuss how picking up on clues in this way provides a good start to developing sensitivity towards others.

VARIATION

Have group members write down a statement about their ambitions, what they want from the group, what they want from their work, what they want from their social life, and so on. Match the statement to the purpose of the group.

COMMENT

Use this activity when group members show a lack of sensitivity towards each other. This exercise can be repeated, asking group members to write a second statement immediately – either later in the same session or a subsequent session. It can be especially useful when the group meets on a regular basis and needs to build rapport.

USE ALSO FOR

Building trust and motivation.

AIMS

↑ To encourage group members to take responsibility for sensitivity towards each other
↑ To raise awareness about how other group members feel
↑ To strengthen the group rapport
↑ To develop sensitivity towards each other

Assessment and evaluation

8

Activities to assess and evaluate the progress of the group as a whole, the individuals within it and the facilitator's performance.

8 Instant feedback

AIMS

↑ To obtain quick feedback on how the session, course, activity or group is going

↑ To enable instant adjustments or adaptations of activities to meet the needs of group members

PREPARATION *materials needed*

Prepare an open question that will encourage feedback or a response that gives you specific information. This can be a question like 'What has been the most important thing you have learned today?' or 'What has been the most difficult and what has been the easiest part of the session for you?' Ensure that the question is phrased to extract the information that you want. Keep it simple and to the point.

THE ACTIVITY

At an appropriate point in the session, explain to the group that you would like their feedback on this activity or session in particular, or on how the sessions are going in general. Having explained this, ask the prepared question and say that you want each person, in turn, to state their reply briefly. Tell the group that there will not be any discussion while participants are making their statements. Allow a couple of minutes for thought and then start the round. Once everyone has responded, you may want to discuss issues raised – or any changes that need to be made in response to the participants' feedback.

VARIATION

Phrase the question so that a simple one – or two – word answer is sufficient and explain that this is all you want. For example, 'Was the task too difficult or too easy?' or 'How difficult was the activity on a scale of 1 to 10?'

COMMENT

This activity is a good way to get an instant response without holding up the progress of the session. It is simple and easy to use and can be used for all types of groups. Detailed discussion of any serious issues exposed may need to be scheduled for a later date to avoid interruption to the current session.

USE ALSO FOR

Building trust, problem solving and managing behaviour and personal responsibility.

Knowledge quiz

PREPARATION *materials needed*

Prepare a quiz based on planned learning for part or all of the session, as appropriate, and obtain some prizes, such as chocolates, pens or diaries – one for each member of the winning team. Obtain some lesser prizes for the losers – such as a bag of sweets to share.

THE ACTIVITY

Inform the group that after the break there will be a fun competition and that prizes will be awarded. Tell them that they must be back in the room on time to compete. When the participants return, split them into small teams. Name or number each team and start the quiz.

Award points for the first team to volunteer a correct answer: award, say, five points for each full answer, three points for part answers, and so on. Ensure that teams explain their answers fully, so that anyone who did not know them will understand.

Each person on the winning team gets a prize. Give lesser prizes to everyone else.

VARIATION

Have everyone compete individually. A quiz works equally well at the end of a session.

COMMENT

This is a fun way to check and reinforce learning.

USE ALSO FOR

Energising and closures.

AIMS

- To review what has been learned
- To energise participants
- To encourage participants back after a break
- To have fun

8 Poster

AIMS
↑ To assess what has been learned
↑ To review main points
↑ To revise the session
↑ To challenge participants

PREPARATION *materials needed*

Have available sheets of drawing paper, magic markers, crayons, coloured pencils and other drawing materials.

THE ACTIVITY

Split participants into small sub-groups. Provide each sub-group with a selection of drawing materials and instruct them to design a poster that shows the key learning points from the session. They can use words, drawings, poetry or symbols to express themselves.

After a set time, bring everyone back together and have each sub-group present and explain its poster.

VARIATION

Instead of creating a poster, have participants create a full-page advertisement for a magazine or newspaper, based on what they have learned during the session or sessions.

COMMENT

This exercise helps learning through visual memory. If asking participants to draw an advertisement, it is useful to have some examples of adverts from magazines available. A good end-of-session activity.

USE ALSO FOR

Energising, stimulating learning, closures.

Good value

PREPARATION *materials needed*

Provide each sub-group with a large sheet of paper and magic markers.

THE ACTIVITY

Group the participants into sub-groups. Ask each group to evaluate the session. Tell them that they must list what they have learned on the sheet of paper and give each learning point a value out of 10.

When each sub-group has completed its task, bring everyone back together again and ask each one, in turn, to give feedback on their findings to the main group. If the sub-groups have given different values out of 10, or have focused on different areas, discuss the reasons for this.

VARIATION

Have participants do the exercise individually or in pairs.

COMMENT

Incorporate the feedback comments in a written evaluation. The comments produced from this type of exercise are likely to be more creative than those generated by more conventional means such as written forms.

USE ALSO FOR

Energising and problem solving.

AIMS

↑ To obtain feedback from the group
↑ To evaluate the session
↑ To review what has been learned

8 Feelings chart

AIMS

↑ To obtain feedback from the group
↑ To provide an opportunity for participants to express how they are feeling
↑ To facilitate discussion
↑ To show progress

PREPARATION *materials needed*

Have some coloured labels available.

THE ACTIVITY

Draw a grid as shown below on a flipchart or whiteboard.

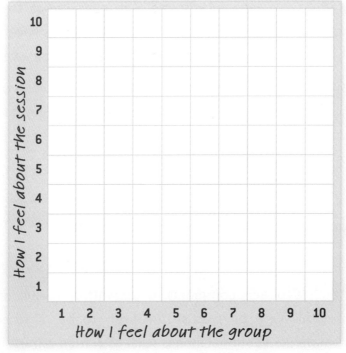

Give each participant a coloured label and ask him to write his name on it. Next, ask each one to think about his feelings and to place his label at an intersection that best represents how he feels both about the group and the session. Each person, in turn, explains why he has placed his label where he did.

Finally, discuss any issues or patterns that the completed chart reveals.

VARIATION

Give each person two labels (different colours), one to place where he feels he is now and one to place at the point he would like to reach. When each person comments on the placing of his labels, discuss ways to close any gaps.

COMMENT

This exercise can be carried out at the beginning of a session, halfway through and then again at the end. Discuss any changes that occur in the pattern. You could also use the chart over a number of sessions, to plot changes.

USE ALSO FOR

Energising, stimulating learning and problem solving.

Agree or disagree?

PREPARATION *materials needed*

Prepare a set of questions based on the topic for the session.

THE ACTIVITY

Ask each participant to respond to one of the prepared questions on the topic covered. The other group members vote on whether they agree or disagree with the answer given. You then discuss any misconceptions and verify the correct answer.

VARIATION

Give each participant a moment to think of a question about the topic, to ask someone else. Participants then take turns at naming a group member and asking him a question. Ensure that each person is asked a question and that any misconceptions are corrected.

COMMENT

This exercise provides instant feedback, enabling you to adapt or plan further sessions as necessary.

USE ALSO FOR

Energising, stimulating learning and problem solving.

AIMS

↑ To assess knowledge gained
↑ To provide instant feedback
↑ To correct any misconceptions

8 Consequences

AIMS

↑ To evaluate what has been learned

↑ To revise what has been learned

↑ To share approaches

↑ To encourage collaboration

PREPARATION *materials needed*

Provide flipchart sheets and magic markers.

THE ACTIVITY

Split participants into pairs. Give each pair a flipchart sheet and a magic marker. Each pair spends a few minutes writing down what they have learned in the session. Each sheet is then passed on to another pair. The new pairs now put a line through anything on the sheet they have received that they did not themselves learn in the session, and add other items they did learn. (Some of what they have written on previous sheets will be repeated.) This continues until each pair has written on each sheet. Each pair then presents the sheet they started with to the whole group. Items which have not been crossed out show what everyone has learned. Crossings out show what needs to be explained again; learning points not mentioned on any sheets will also need revisiting.

VARIATION

Use at the beginning of a session to assess what is known by participants about a particular topic.

COMMENT

If a question or problem is posed to the group, use the same procedure: it will help the participants to come up with different arguments or to suggest the elements to be considered. The 'fun' element aids creative thought.

USE ALSO FOR

Stimulating learning, motivation and problem solving.

Reaction sheets

PREPARATION *materials needed*

Have large sheets of paper prepared, showing the questions that you will use to elicit comments from the participants. Examples might be: 'What would you change?', 'What worked best for you?', 'What was the least useful?' and so on. Also have available a supply of sticky labels or adhesive notes.

THE ACTIVITY

Display the prepared sheets of paper. Hand out plenty of sticky labels and ask participants to put under each question asked at least one sticker with their answers written on it.

VARIATION

Divide the group members into pairs or small groups to discuss the questions and to place sticky notes, with their combined comments on, on each sheet.

COMMENT

The comments gathered can be compiled into a formal evaluation and the issues addressed in follow-up sessions.

USE ALSO FOR

Problem solving and closures.

AIMS

↑ To evaluate the session or programme

↑ To provide a light and relaxed end to the session

↑ To stimulate creative thought

8 Reflection time

AIMS

↑ To encourage reflection on what has been learned

↑ To identify what has been gained personally

↑ To examine what has changed

↑ To build confidence

PREPARATION *materials needed*

Prepare a form asking participants what they want from the course. Ask them to write down four personal aims for the course or prompt them with sentence beginnings based on the course objectives, as shown below.

My aims for these sessions are:

→ *to be able to ...*

→ *to know ...*

→ *to feel ...*

Have pens available for participants' use during the session.

THE ACTIVITY

At the beginning of the session or course, invite participants to fill in a simple form stating what they want from the course, as described above. This can be completed individually or in pairs. At the end of the session have everyone discuss in pairs, sub-groups or as a whole group what they have achieved or learned in relation to their original completed forms. Finish by having each person make a statement saying:

→ What he is now able to do

→ What he now knows

→ What he now feels

VARIATION

Revisit each participant's personal goals for the session and then facilitate a discussion in pairs, sub-groups or as a whole group, about what has been achieved or learned. Finish by inviting each person to state two things personal to them that they have learned and now use, or will use in the future.

COMMENT

If using sentence beginnings, adapt these to suit the session or group aims as necessary.

USE ALSO FOR

Energising, stimulating learning and motivation.

Moving on

PREPARATION *materials needed*

Provide pens and paper.

THE ACTIVITY

Break the group into pairs or small sub-groups. Ask each sub-group to discuss any change in how they think or behave or in whatever skills the group might focus on. How have the participants' skills improved or changed? In the light of any changes, group members then discuss what their goals are for the future and what their first step will be towards achieving them. Participants' goals might now be:

AIMS

↑ To reflect on what has changed

↑ To acknowledge any change

↑ To plan for the future

→ to get a voluntary job

→ to do a computer course

→ to organise their time better

→ to say 'no' when they do not want to do something

→ to put a newly learned skill into practice

Alternatively, participants might want to modify original goals. After a set time for discussion, bring the group together again and invite participants to state a goal and what their first step towards achieving it will be.

VARIATION

After discussion in pairs or sub-groups, have group members write out a step-by-step action plan that will help them to achieve their goal. Participants then share these plans with the whole group.

COMMENT

If the group plans to meet after a month to review how everyone has been getting on, written action plans can be used as a focus for the meeting.

USE ALSO FOR

Energising and motivation.

8 Expert

AIMS

↑ To assess knowledge
↑ To encourage participation
↑ To help participants learn from each other
↑ To make the session fun

PREPARATION *materials needed*

Provide sheets of paper and pens and a hat or cap with the word 'expert' written on it.

THE ACTIVITY

Hand out paper and pens. Introduce the session topic or topics and ask participants to make notes about what they know about the topic. This might be a technique or a process, for example. After a set time, ask everyone to sit in a circle.

Invite a volunteer to wear the cap and explain what he knows about the topic. Other group members can ask questions but the 'expert' can say, 'Pass!' if he does not know the answer. When the expert has said all he wants to on the subject, another volunteer takes the cap to add additional points, and so on.

You take notes on anything said that is incorrect or will need further explanation and on anything that has been missed. These notes are added at the end, as part of a summary of what has been shared.

VARIATION

If some group members lack confidence, invite them to write their notes in pairs or in small sub-groups.

COMMENT

Use this activity at the beginning or end of a session, to assess knowledge or to evaluate participants' understanding of what has been covered.

USE ALSO FOR

Energising, stimulating learning and motivation.

My performance

PREPARATION *materials needed*

Draw on a board or flipchart a diagram as shown below. Each column, numbered on the horizontal axis, represents one of the participants: adjust the chart according to the number of participants in your group.

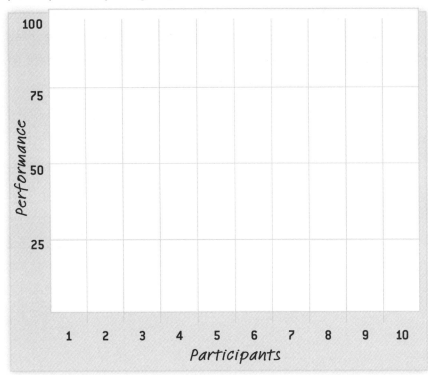

Provide pens, paper and magic markers.

THE ACTIVITY

Tell the group members that you are going to leave the room, leaving the chart on display. While you are out of the room, the participants are to allocate between them the numbers from the horizontal axis, so that each participant has a different number. Each participant then draws a line on the chart, within his own column, rating your performance as a group facilitator on a scale from 0 to 100. When participants have finished, they have a brief discussion and make notes on why individuals have placed the performance lines on different levels.

After this discussion, the group chooses one or two spokespersons who will explain the group's conclusions to you, the group facilitator. You then come back in the room, look at the chart and listen to the elected spokesperson. Ask questions about the ratings, but avoid putting anyone on the spot. If the spokesperson is unable to answer, any group member can join in if they wish.

AIMS

- ↑ To obtain feedback on performance
- ↑ To give participants an opportunity to say if their expectations have been met
- ↑ To address any unrealistic expectations
- ↑ To raise awareness of the facilitator as to how they are seen by group members

VARIATION

Provide each participant with a prepared chart to fill in and have the charts returned to you anonymously – for example, you might ask a participant to collect and return the forms to you.

COMMENT

You will need to pick up on any issues and address them. The charts may sometimes show the existence of a problem without identifying it. It may not be appropriate to pursue the issue at the time; instead you should follow it up later.

USE ALSO FOR

Building trust and problem solving.

Mid-session check-up

PREPARATION *materials needed*

Prepare a simple questionnaire, for example:

1 What do you like so far?
2 What do you dislike?
3 What would you like included that has not been covered?
4 What has been included that you think is not necessary?
5 What questions would you like to ask?
6 What do you feel uncomfortable with?
7 What would you like changed?

Have pens available.

THE ACTIVITY

Hand out the questionnaires and invite participants to complete them. It is usually best to do this before a break. This gives you time to go through the completed forms and decide on any necessary action for the rest of the session. When participants gather again as a group, explain what adjustments you plan to make as a result of their feedback. If the questionnaires are completed at the end of a session, action needs to be decided and explained at the beginning of the next session.

VARIATION

The questions can be discussed as a large group and notes taken by the group leader, or the questionnaires may be filled in in pairs or in small groups.

COMMENT

Thank the group for their feedback and share with them any action that you have decided on. If they are perfectly happy and do not want any changes, share that with them too.

USE ALSO FOR

Energising, stimulating learning, motivation and problem solving.

AIMS

↑ To obtain feedback midway through a session or course
↑ To provide an opportunity for participants to ask questions that they might not ask verbally
↑ To check if anything has been missed
↑ To enable adjustments to be made to meet individual needs

8 Initial assessment sentences

AIMS

↑ To gain knowledge of participants' relevant skills and experience

↑ To enable adjustments to be made to the session or sessions to meet individual needs

↑ To encourage participants to disclose and share their experience

PREPARATION *materials needed*

Prepare a simple questionnaire with statements for completion. For example:

1 My experience of … includes …

2 The relevant skills I have are …

3 What I find difficult is …

4 What I want to learn is …

Have pens available. You will need flipchart sheets and magic markers for the variation.

THE ACTIVITY

Distribute the questionnaire and allow participants a set time to complete it. Depending on the circumstances of your group, it may be possible to ask participants to complete the questionnaire prior to the session. Ask for volunteers to share what they have written with the whole group. As participants state what they want to learn or find difficult, you can note areas of difficulty to focus on and confirm that these will be covered. You will also be made aware of the group's skills and experiences, which you can make use of during the session. Finish by collecting the forms for future reference.

VARIATION

Split the participants into pairs or small groups to discuss experience, skills, difficulties and to find out what they want to learn. Then ask the participants to give feedback to the complete group, making notes on flipchart sheets under the different headings.

COMMENT

An activity that is really effective – not only in providing information, but also in breaking down barriers, exposing shared interests and helping the group members to build trust.

USE ALSO FOR

Building trust, stimulating learning, motivation and problem solving.

Noughts and crosses

PREPARATION *materials needed*

Prepare a quiz based on the topic or material used in the session. You may add novelty by giving sweets to the teams that win each round. Provide a chalkboard and chalk or a whiteboard or flipchart and magic marker.

AIMS

↑ To review what has been learned

↑ To revise the key concepts

↑ To make the process fun

THE ACTIVITY

Form the group members into two teams and draw a noughts and crosses chart on the board or flipchart. Decide which team will be 'noughts' and which 'crosses'. Toss a coin to see who will answer the first question. If a team gets a question right they choose where to put their '0' or 'X'; if the team gets the question wrong, it can be passed to the opposing team. If neither get it right, you can provide the correct answer.

VARIATION

Prepare a simple crossword, with clues that define key concept words. The crossword can then be completed by the group.

COMMENT

Although some effort is needed to compile puzzles or write questions for these games, the fun and enthusiasm generated makes the hard work well worth while.

USE ALSO FOR

Stimulating learning, motivation and closures.

Additional tools

More activities that will help you to manage your group effectively. Includes activities on forming sub-groups, obtaining feedback and encouraging self-awareness.

9 All in a line

AIMS

↑ To divide group members into pairs or sub-groups

↑ To provide a random mix of participants

↑ To energise participants

PREPARATION *materials needed*

None.

THE ACTIVITY

Instruct the group members to form a line, with the shortest person on the left and the tallest on the right. Have everyone call out what number they are, starting with number one on the left. If you want pairs, have odd numbers pair with even numbers. If you want groups of three, have numbers one to three as one group, numbers four to six as another group, and so on. If you want two groups, have odd numbers as one group and even numbers as another group. Many different combinations can be formed in this way.

VARIATION

Instruct the participants to form a line in alphabetical order, using either first names or family names. Participants can then be broken into whatever combination is appropriate to any activity or purpose.

COMMENT

This procedure avoids the same people repeatedly forming into groups, encourages mixing and helps the participants to learn from others with different experiences and backgrounds.

USE ALSO FOR

Building trust and energising.

What sort of group?

9

PREPARATION *materials needed*

None.

THE ACTIVITY

Ask participants to think of the group as an animal. What species of animal would best represent it? Would it be an elephant that lumbers along, a doe that is frightened of confrontation, a tiger that strides fearlessly through the issues addressed, or some other animal that displays different characteristics? After a moment for thought, ask each group member, in turn, to say which animal the group most resembles, and why.

Make notes as people make their statements; discuss what has been learned, including any surprises, and address any issues highlighted.

VARIATION

Replace animals with flowers, fish, fruits or objects.

COMMENT

This exercise can be used at various stages of the group's development to obtain a picture of how individuals view the changes that have occurred.

USE ALSO FOR

Energising, problem solving and assessment and evaluation.

AIMS

↑ To discover how group members view the group

↑ To bring out both negative and positive images of the group

↑ To raise participants' awareness of the impact of what is happening in the group on each other

9 Nicknames

AIMS

↑ To introduce people to each other

↑ To break down barriers

↑ To lighten the tone of the session

↑ To energise group members

↑ To encourage disclosures

↑ To have fun

PREPARATION *materials needed*

None.

THE ACTIVITY

Ask each group member, in turn, to disclose a nickname they had – when at school or as a child, at work, with a partner or at home. Ask them how they got the nickname and why. If using this as an introductory activity, have each person state his name before disclosing the nickname.

VARIATION

Ask each participant to describe one of his weaknesses and one of his strengths. Then ask them to say why they perceive them as such. In each case, discuss when the weakness might become a strength.

COMMENT

This is a useful multipurpose exercise that can be used at different times in a session.

USE ALSO FOR

Building trust and energising.

Find your partner

PREPARATION *materials needed*

Prepare slips of paper or cards with a sport written on each card: for example weightlifting, tennis, swimming, ice skating, bowling, cricket, and so on. If you want to split the group into pairs, two cards must show the same sport; if you want groups of four, four cards must be the same, and so on.

THE ACTIVITY

Hand out the cards at random and instruct the participants to keep secret what is written on their card. When everyone has a card, tell them that you want them to form into pairs or small groups: in order to find their partner or partners, they have to circulate and mime the sport written on the card. No-one is allowed to speak during this activity.

VARIATION

Substitute jobs, activities or hobbies for sport.

COMMENT

Another simple activity to avoid people sticking with the same partner or sub-group. This activity encourages mixing and learning from others with different backgrounds.

USE ALSO FOR

Introductions and icebreakers and energising.

AIMS

↑ To divide the group into pairs or small groups
↑ To energise group members
↑ To break down barriers
↑ To encourage mixing
↑ To have fun

9 Learning from life

AIMS

↑ To help group members identify how they learn from experience

↑ To choose an event from life and reflect on what has been learned from it

↑ To break down barriers

↑ To encourage disclosure and learning from each other

PREPARATION *materials needed*

Prepare statement sheets for each participant as follows.

→ *Because of what happened I ...*

→ *I am now ...*

→ *I feel ...*

→ *I know ...*

Prior to using the variation you will need to prepare a case study (as described below) and to provide pens for participants' use.

THE ACTIVITY

Ask group members to think of an experience they have had in life. They may think of it as either good or bad. It could be moving house, changing jobs, being made redundant, working as a volunteer, looking after a family member, a holiday romance, an argument at work with a colleague, falling out with a friend, and so on.

Divide the group into pairs and have partners tell each other about their experiences. Together they reflect on their experiences and what they learned from them; they then complete the statement sheets. For example:

→ Because of what happened I ... (take responsibility for myself)

→ I am now ... (more able on cope on my own)

→ I feel ... (more confident)

→ I know ... (how to budget so I don't get into debt)

Complete the exercise by bringing everyone back together and having them share the different things they have learned from their experiences.

VARIATION

Put together a case study of a particular experience. This can be loosely based on an experience of your own. Relate the experience to the group, discuss what could be learned from it and complete a statement sheet together. Then ask the group members to reflect on an experience of their own and share one thing that they learned from it.

COMMENT

This exercise demonstrates that life is a continuous learning experience in which people acquire new skills and develop personally. Mistakes and failures provide us with new opportunities for learning.

USE ALSO FOR

Building trust and stimulating learning.

9 Ground rules

AIMS

- To set ground rules
- To agree how to create a safe and productive environment
- To establish what is and is not acceptable
- To encourage participants to take personal responsibility for their own behaviour and learning
- To build trust

PREPARATION *materials needed*

Have a flipchart available and a large sheet of paper and magic markers for each group.

THE ACTIVITY

Split the group into sub-groups and have each one answer the following questions:

→ What do you expect from each other during the sessions?

→ What do you want from the group leader?

→ What can you do to make the group successful?

→ What routine rules do you need to agree concerning issues such as punctuality and confidentiality?

Each sub-group writes their conclusions on a large sheet of paper using the magic markers and then, in turn, presents them to the whole group. The information presented is discussed and the group decides on the ground rules for the group sessions.

VARIATION

Invite the participants to write their answers to the questions on adhesive notes and post these on a board. The answers can then be discussed one at a time and general guidelines agreed with the group.

COMMENT

This activity is best completed after people have been introduced and are getting to know each other. Guidelines agreed in this way help to prevent any problems developing and assist in the building of trust.

USE ALSO FOR

Building trust, motivation and managing behaviour and personal responsibility.

Forming sub-groups

PREPARATION *materials needed*

Prepare a deck of cards with numbers equal to the number of people in the group.

THE ACTIVITY

Shuffle the deck and have each group member choose a card. Instruct the group how you want them to form sub-groups. For example, you might ask all even numbers and all odd numbers to work together, or numbers one to four, five to eight and nine to twelve to work together, and so on, depending on the requirements of the activity planned; many different combinations may be used. The cards can be retrieved, reshuffled and new groups formed at any time.

VARIATION

Instead of forming the groups using numbered cards use cards showing the letters of the alphabet or have people pick out different coloured pieces of paper from a bag.

COMMENT

This avoids the same people always working together, encourages mixing and helps the participants to learn from others with different backgrounds.

USE ALSO FOR

Energising and stimulating learning.

AIMS

↑ To perform specific tasks

↑ To discuss how learning about a topic may apply to group members

↑ To share and generate ideas

↑ To work on a task

↑ To involve group members in a process

↑ To support each other

9 The group is like ...

↑ To obtain feedback
from participants
about how they see
the group
↑ To discover the
negative and positive
images of the group,
as seen by the group
↑ To encourage
awareness
↑ To bring out any
hidden issues

PREPARATION *materials needed*

None.

THE ACTIVITY

Each group member makes a statement beginning with 'The group is like …' and explains the meaning if it is not immediately obvious. For example, someone might say, 'The group is like a balloon about to burst'. Further exploration might reveal that the person feels there is anger building in the group and fears that it might explode at any time, or it might just be how that person feels. A more positive group experience might elicit the statement: 'The group is like a comfortable warm blanket'. Of course, that could mean that the group, depending on its purpose, is too cosy or comfortable and that people are not being challenged.

After everyone has made their statements, discuss with the participants how they feel and talk through any surprises that have emerged.

VARIATION

Change the opening statement to 'When I visualise the group I feel …'.

COMMENT

Ensure that any issues that emerge are addressed. Some issues may need to be deferred to a special slot because of their importance or because it would be difficult to deal with them on the spot. Some issues may be personal to individuals and may need to be addressed with that individual after the group session.

USE ALSO FOR

Problem solving and assessment and evaluation.

Action and reaction

PREPARATION *materials needed*

Have available a flipchart to make notes on.

THE ACTIVITY

Ask group members to reflect on a recent action that they have taken – it may be something within the group or in their personal life. It might be that a person has decided to study or to give up their job and start a small business from home. It may be some small action like laying down a rule that everyone in the family takes turns at washing up. Use a shared, real example or one of the above fictional examples as a case study: discuss the reactions that these actions could generate for other people.

Afterwards discuss as a group the following questions:

→ Why is it important to think about other people's reactions and to talk to them about these reactions?

→ What impact might these reactions have on your relationships if you do not discuss them?

→ Does everyone have a responsibility to anticipate reactions and to discuss in advance the action with those it might affect?

VARIATION

Split into sub-groups to reflect and discuss possible reactions to an action taken and bring everyone back together again to discuss the questions.

COMMENT

Often an action taken by someone in the group will have affected the group either positively or negatively, and this can be used as a case study.

USE ALSO FOR

Motivation, problem solving and managing behaviour and personal responsibility.

AIMS

↑ To make group members aware that any actions they take will impact on others

↑ To raise awareness of how their actions may be interpreted by others

↑ To predict reaction to actions

↑ To alter actions to allow for anticipated reactions

↑ To help plan actions to achieve goals

9 How was it for you?

AIMS

⬆ To review how participants have put into practice learning from a previous session

⬆ To share experiences and support each other

⬆ To get to know each other better

⬆ To bring out any misconceptions from previous learning

PREPARATION *materials needed*

Provide pens and paper.

THE ACTIVITY

Split the group into pairs. Instruct the partners to talk to each other and share progress on tasks set or on putting their learning into practice since the previous session. Ask them to make notes. After a few minutes, bring everyone back together in a large group. Each person then explains what their partner has done or how they have implemented what was learned in the previous session. You can pick up on any issues that emerge.

VARIATION

To shorten the time, have each participant, in turn, share with the whole group how they have progressed.

COMMENT

A simple exercise that sets the expectation that learning will be put into practice.

USE ALSO FOR

Stimulating learning, problem solving and assessment and evaluation.

Session link

PREPARATION *materials needed*

Have a flipchart and magic markers available.

THE ACTIVITY

Ask each participant, in turn, to state either something that they learned or that was important to them from the last session. List these statements on a flipchart and summarise. Remind the group of any points that have been omitted. Any important items that are missing from the list may need to be scheduled into the programme again.

VARIATION

Have the group members, in turn, complete statements such as the following:

→ After the last session I felt … (I needed to change my attitude)

→ One thing I learned from the last session was that … (it is possible to organise my day in a different way)

→ What I remember from the last session is … (how to control my breathing when I am beginning to feel anxious)

COMMENT

Statements like these can be changed to meet the needs of most groups and provide continuity from one session to another. Paired statements can be used, such as:

→ What I learned from *the last* session was …

→ What I want from *this* session is …

USE ALSO FOR

Introductions and icebreakers, motivation and problem solving.

AIMS

↑ To remind participants of what has been gained from a previous session

↑ To provide an indication of how individuals are feeling at the start of a session

↑ To obtain feedback about what has been remembered from a previous session

↑ To summarise previous learning

↑ To provide an icebreaker

9 True or false?

AIMS

↑ To revise material previously learned

↑ To assess what has been learned so far

↑ To involve everyone

PREPARATION *materials needed*

Make up two sets of cards: one set should comprise questions based on the session topics and the other answers to these questions. Some of the answers should be incorrect. Blank cards and pens will be needed for the variation.

THE ACTIVITY

Shuffle the cards and deal them at random to the group members. Ask a participant who has a question to read the question aloud. Whoever thinks that their card gives the answer then reads this out. The group then votes on whether this answer is true or false. If the group decides the answer is false, ask if anyone knows the correct answer: if so, have them explain it. If no-one knows the answer, you may step in and provide it. Continue in this way until all the cards have been used.

VARIATION

Hand out two blank cards to each participant. Each person then writes a question card and an answer card. These are collected and shuffled and handed out again at random. Ask someone with a question card to read it out and proceed as above.

COMMENT

This activity is a novel way of revising or assessing what has been learned.

USE ALSO FOR

Energising, stimulating learning and assessment and evaluation.

Crash

PREPARATION *materials needed*

Chairs, tables and other furniture can be used to represent the various obstacles described below.

THE ACTIVITY

Form small groups of four or five people. Ask them to imagine that their plane has crashed in a dangerous and remote place. They can only take one thing each from the plane, scattered luggage and debris to help them find their way to safety. On their journey they must climb a steep rock-face, traverse a wide and fast-flowing river, wade through a swamp made more hazardous by quicksand and crocodiles, and cross a chasm to reach safety. The group should first decide what each person will take with him. Both the journey and how to overcome the obstacles it presents should be planned and acted out as if they were really happening.

When all the sub-groups have completed their journeys discuss:

→ what they chose to take on the journey and why

→ how they overcame obstacles

→ how they made decisions

→ how well participants cooperated with each other

→ how individuals felt during the experience

AIMS

↑ To encourage people to work together

↑ To explore problem solving and decision making

↑ To aid the group bonding process

↑ To stimulate imagination

↑ To have fun

VARIATION

Have group members imagine that they have been taken prisoner and abandoned in a remote place; they must find their way to safety by overcoming the obstacles.

COMMENT

The obstacles can be changed to suit the group.

USE ALSO FOR

Building trust, energising and problem solving.

9 Adapting to change

AIMS

↑ To stimulate thought about change and its effects

↑ To introduce the process of making changes

↑ To explore the feelings experienced when adapting to change

↑ To demonstrate the difficulties involved when making changes

↑ To break down barriers

PREPARATION *materials needed*

Provide paper and pencils for each participant.

THE ACTIVITY

Ask the participants to choose an object: for example, a desk, a tree, a car or a lawnmower. Distribute paper and pencils and ask participants to draw their objects using the hand not normally used.

When this has been completed each participant, in turn, shows his drawing to the group who try to guess what it is.

Then ask the group the following questions:

➡ Who felt uncomfortable using a different hand?

➡ Is this typical of feelings experienced even making simple changes?

➡ How can this obstacle to change be overcome?

VARIATION

Ask group members to think of a few simple tasks that they perform regularly, like making a cup of tea or getting dressed in the morning. Get them to perform these actions in the normal order and then change the order in which they carry out each step.

COMMENT

People normally feel uncomfortable with change because of their uncertainty of the outcome. This activity will help participants to look objectively at their uncertainty. The activity is also good to use as a fun ice breaker and can be used as a demonstration of difficulties that might be faced in bringing about a change of some kind.

USE ALSO FOR

Introductions and icebreakers, energising and motivation.

Interviews

PREPARATION *materials needed*

Have in mind a number of topics based on the session. Write the topics on slips of paper and place them in a bag. For example, in a session about shyness, topics might include: what loneliness feels like, how shyness affects people, ways in which shyness can be overcome, and so on. One topic is needed for each group member.

THE ACTIVITY

The participants sit in a circle and a volunteer is asked to choose the first topic from a bag. This participant reads out his topic and is then asked questions about it by the other group members. You should be ready to support anyone who gets into difficulty answering questions and to step in when an incorrect answer is given. The activity continues until every group member has had a go.

Finish the activity by discussing with everyone how they felt about being interviewed and summarising what was covered.

VARIATION

Have participants write down five questions that they could ask someone about the session. They then pair up with another participant and, using the prepared questions, the partners interview each other about what has been learned. Finish the activity by discussing with the group what came up in the interviews and how they felt.

COMMENT

A fun way to revise learning.

USE ALSO FOR

Energising and assessment and evaluation.

Closures

Activities for bringing a session or series of sessions to an end.

10 Mentor

AIMS

- To close the session or sessions
- To reflect on learning
- To reinforce learning
- To review what has been learned
- To share learning
- To look at the difficulties of putting learning into practice

PREPARATION *materials needed*

None.

THE ACTIVITY

Divide the group into pairs and have them decide who is going to be 'A' and who 'B'. For five minutes 'A' mentors or coaches 'B', helping him to overcome any difficulties he may have in putting into practice what he has learned. Then 'B' coaches 'A' in the same way. After a set time bring the group back together to share anticipated difficulties and solutions.

VARIATION

Have 'A' explain to 'B' how he plans to put his learning into practice. 'B' thinks up as many difficulties as he can and helps 'A' to think of solutions should they arise. 'B' then explains to 'A' how he plans to put his learning into practice, and so on. Finally, possible difficulties and solutions are shared with the whole large group.

COMMENT

This activity demonstrates an expectation that learning will be implemented and encourages individuals to make changes. It can be backed up by feedback in a later session or by arranging for the group to meet again for feedback.

USE ALSO FOR

Energising, motivation and problem solving.

Letter of commitment

10

PREPARATION *materials needed*

Provide an envelope, a pen and paper for each participant.

THE ACTIVITY

Have the group members write a letter to themselves, about the group. Ask them to list ways of implementing what they have learned. They should also write about any problems that they foresee, and their possible solutions. They then address the envelope to themselves and seal it.

The letters can be posted to the group members on an agreed date. Alternatively, you can arrange for the group to meet again at a future date to open the envelopes and share experiences.

VARIATION

Divide the group members into pairs. They discuss how they are going to implement what has been learned, possible difficulties and solutions to them. Then each participant writes his letter to himself.

COMMENT

Another good way of encouraging individuals to implement learning or changes they have resolved to make.

USE ALSO FOR

Motivation, problem solving and managing behaviour and personal responsibility.

AIMS

↑ To close the session or sessions

↑ To encourage participants to implement what they have learned

↑ To identify ways of putting learning into practice

↑ To follow up on learning

↑ To encourage individuals to set themselves targets

Gifts

AIMS

↑ To close the session or sessions

↑ To ensure a 'feel good' feeling at the end of the session

↑ To boost self-esteem

↑ To encourage positive feelings between group members

PREPARATION *materials needed*

Prepare small cards or pieces of paper with a group members' name written on each, sticky labels and pens.

THE ACTIVITY

Place the name cards in a bag and invite group members to pick out one each. Participants then think of a gift to give the person named – based on their knowledge of them as gained during the session. They also prepare a statement to accompany the gift: for example, 'I appreciate the feedback you gave me during the last activity. It was really helpful. I would like to give you a trip to Tokyo to see your brother'. Allow a moment for people to decide on the gift they plan to give and then ask them, one at a time, to make their statements.

VARIATION

Hand out lots of sticky labels and ask group members to write a brief statement of appreciation and thanks to each of the other members of the group. They then circulate and stick their labels on each other. Finally, group members read aloud their notes of appreciation.

COMMENT

It is surprising just how much these statements can mean to participants when verbalised in this way.

USE ALSO FOR

Building trust, energising and motivation.

Message board

PREPARATION *materials needed*

Prepare three flipchart sheets with the following headings, one heading on each sheet:

1 How I feel

2 Something/someone I appreciated during the session

3 What I learned

Have available a good supply of sticky notes and pens.

THE ACTIVITY

Display the prepared flipcharts sheets. Hand out the sticky notes and pens. Then ask each person to write at least one sticky label for each titled sheet and to stick their labels on the appropriate sheets. When this has been completed, read out what has been written on each of the sheets in turn.

VARIATION

Substitute or add to the labelled sheets to suit the group purpose. Other useful titles you might include could be:

→ What I now want to know is …

→ What I am going to do now is …

COMMENT

Participants tend to feel comfortable with this method of feedback and it is fun to use.

USE ALSO FOR

Energising, motivation, problem solving and assessment and evaluation.

AIMS
↑ To close the session or sessions
↑ To find out what has been learned
↑ To give positive feedback to group members
↑ To find out how group members are feeling

10 Planning for the future

AIMS

↑ To close the session or sessions

↑ To enable participants to put their learning into practice

↑ To reflect on what has been learned

↑ To obtain feedback on how well each person has learned

PREPARATION *materials needed*

Have available sheets of paper and pens.

THE ACTIVITY

Hand out the paper and pens. Ask participants to reflect on their learning in the session and to produce a written action plan for carrying it through into their lives. For example, if the session was on 'stress' they could write down how they are going to manage an event they find stressful; if the session was on 'getting organised' they could state how they are going to organise their diary, desk or time.

When the task has been completed, each person shares their action plan with the group.

VARIATION

Divide the group into pairs or small groups to help each other reflect on their learning and plan how to put it into practice. Each person then shares his plans with the whole group.

COMMENT

It is important that people state their intentions for action. Stating them in this way gives a better commitment to actually carrying them out.

USE ALSO FOR

Energising, stimulating learning, assessment and evaluation.

Before I leave

PREPARATION *materials needed*

None.

THE ACTIVITY

Form the group into a circle and invite the participants, one by one, to complete the statement 'Before I leave …'. They might say:

→ *I would like to thank everybody for being such good company*

→ *I would like to thank you for giving me so much support when I was struggling*

→ *I would like to thank Peter for his kindness and help getting here each week*

→ *I would like to thank Jean for her patience and for being such a good listener when I needed to talk.*

VARIATION

Have group members complete a sentence beginning, 'I appreciate …'.

COMMENT

This is a simple exercise that leaves participants with positive feelings. Prior to doing the round of statements, it is helpful to remind participants about enjoyable events they have shared or times when they have helped each other.

USE ALSO FOR

Building trust, energising and motivation.

AIMS

↑ To bring the session or sessions to a close
↑ To provide an opportunity for everybody to say goodbye
↑ To ensure everyone leaves with positive feelings

10 Buddies

AIMS

- To provide support after the group is finished
- To aid the transfer of learning into practice
- To support each other
- To encourage and motivate each other
- To help integration with other learning

PREPARATION *materials needed*

None.

THE ACTIVITY

Ask participants to pair up with a partner of their choice (or to group themselves in threes or fours if you prefer). Have the pairs discuss how they will support each other in the future, after the group sessions are finished. For example, they phone each other, meet for a coffee or write to each other to check on progress. Pairs or sub-groups then share with the whole group what they have decided.

'Buddy' partnerships can also be formed early in the life of the group. The pairs or sub-groups discuss how they are going to support each other during and between sessions. This can include having a set routine for phoning each other when they need to talk or meeting between, before or after sessions.

VARIATION

To ensure progress is maintained in the future it is always helpful to have a meeting of the entire group after a set period to share progress and discuss difficulties and possible solutions.

COMMENT

You will need to be aware of any problems that might surface with buddies and to help them overcome or resolve any difficulties. Ensure that buddies are aware that you are available to be consulted.

USE ALSO FOR

Stimulating learning, motivation and problem solving.

What I wanted ...

PREPARATION *materials needed*

Have available a flipchart, magic markers, pens and paper.

THE ACTIVITY

Write the following statement starters on the flipchart:

→ What I wanted from the group today was …

→ What I got from the group today was …

→ What I want from the group in future is …

Give each person, in turn, an opportunity to complete each statement verbally. When this has been done, encourage general discussion about the completed statements.

VARIATION

Split the group into three or four sub-groups. Give them time to discuss the statement beginnings and write down a combined response on paper. Circulate as necessary to give support. When the task has been completed, bring everyone back together and invite an elected person from each sub-group to give feedback to the whole group.

COMMENT

Group leaders must ensure that they respond to the problems and needs identified. Doing this exercise at the end of a session enables group members to feel that they can influence what happens in the group.

USE ALSO FOR

Stimulating learning, motivation and problem solving.

AIMS

↑ To bring the session to a close

↑ To obtain feedback about how the session has gone

↑ To gain knowledge about requirements for future sessions

↑ To obtain information that will help you adapt the sessions to meet expectations

10 Commitment

↑ To provide a sense of closure for the session

↑ To aid integration of material

↑ To encourage a sense of commitment

PREPARATION *materials needed*

Provide a soft ball that can be thrown and caught by group members. Pens and paper will be needed for the variation.

THE ACTIVITY

Ask group members to think about what they are going to commit themselves to do before the next session or after the group has ended. For example, they could be asked to make a statement such as: 'The three things I am going to do between now and the next session are …'.

After allowing a few moments for thought, throw the ball to a group member who makes their commitment statement. He then throws the ball to someone else, who makes a statement. This continues until everyone has been included.

VARIATION

Ask each participant to write on a sheet of paper his name and his statement of commitment. These commitments are then read out and handed in. At the next meeting they are read out again and the person says how they have got on with carrying out their commitment.

COMMENT

This activity sets a clear expectation that learning will be put into practice. If used at the end of a series of sessions then the statement will need to be altered to, 'The three things I am going to do in the future are …'. The statement is adaptable to meet the requirements of most groups.

USE ALSO FOR

Energising and motivation.

What I know

PREPARATION *materials needed*

Have available some flipchart sheets and magic markers.

THE ACTIVITY

Divide the group into pairs. The couples decide who is going to be 'A' and who 'B'. The 'A's explain all they have learned so far. The 'B's pretend to know nothing. After a set time the 'A's pretend to know nothing and the 'B's explain all they have learned, including anything that has been missed by the 'A's. You move around the pairs, correcting any incorrect explanations.

AIMS

↑ To bring the session to a close

↑ To reinforce learning

↑ To revise the session

↑ To reflect on what has been learned

VARIATION

Divide the group into small groups of three or four participants. Using a flipchart sheet, each group puts together a short synopsis of what has been learned. The participants are all brought together again and a spokesperson for each group goes through their synopsis.

COMMENT

Repeating learning makes it more likely that what is learnt will be retained. This activity makes repetition fun and neatly brings the session to a close.

USE ALSO FOR

Stimulating learning and assessment and evaluation.

Mental rehearsal

AIMS

↑ To bring the session or sessions to a close

↑ To encourage group members to act on learning

↑ To build confidence in applying learning

↑ To ensure that everyone feels relaxed

PREPARATION *materials needed*

Have available some soft and relaxing music.

THE ACTIVITY

Ensure that everyone is sitting comfortably and that their clothes are loose. Switch on the music and tell everyone to close their eyes. Say, 'Think of something relaxing'. This may be the sound of the sea, a word like 'calm', a picture they like, a place such as a waterfall or stream, a quiet country scene or a flower. 'As you concentrate, feel your muscles and bodies relaxing. Tension is draining away from your forehead, eyes, mouth and jaw, through the neck, shoulders, down your chest and back, through your arms and from your fingertips. Tension is sinking through your hips, thighs, calves, feet and toes into the floor.'

Remind everyone to concentrate on their own relaxing scene and then repeat the instructions slowly. When you have finished, ask everyone to sit quietly for a moment and reflect on the session and any plan of action they have formulated. Ask them to imagine themselves carrying the plan out and succeeding in their objective.

After a few moments ask the participants to gradually open their eyes, still sitting quietly, and slowly reorientate themselves to the room. Do not allow anyone to stand up or move around immediately.

VARIATION

For some groups, simply playing some soft music for a few minutes and asking everyone to close their eyes and relax is a good way to end a group session.

COMMENT

This is an excellent way to build confidence and encourage participants to carry out an action plan.

USE ALSO FOR

Motivation.

Action statements

PREPARATION *materials needed*

Write the following on a flipchart sheet:

→ *I have learned …*

→ *I am going to …*

→ *Difficulties I see are …*

THE ACTIVITY

Arrange everyone in a circle. Each person, in turn, then makes action statements beginning, 'I have learned …', 'I am going to …', 'Difficulties I see are …'. If a participant's statement suggests that he has problems or barriers, encourage suggestions from the other group members on how these might be overcome.

VARIATION

Split the group into pairs or small groups to discuss their action statements and then have them feed back to the whole group, seated in a large circle.

COMMENT

If using this exercise during a series of sessions be sure to get feedback at the next session on how everyone has got on.

USE ALSO FOR

Motivation, problem solving and assessment and evaluation.

AIMS

↑ To end the session or sessions

↑ To encourage participants to put learning into action

↑ To reinforce learning

↑ To help integration of material

↑ To plan changes

 # Speaking out

AIMS

↑ To bring the session or sessions to an end

↑ To obtain feedback from participants

↑ To reflect on time spent together

↑ To provide an opportunity for participants to express their views

PREPARATION *materials needed*

Write on separate pieces of paper the beginning of a statement relating to the time spent together. You will need one statement for each group member, for example:

→ What interested me most was …

→ What I disliked most was …

→ The funniest thing was …

→ What made me smile was …

→ The person I would like to get to know better is …

→ I was irritated when …

→ I was nervous when …

→ What I would like to do more of is …

→ What helped me most was …

→ The person kindest to me was …

You will need pens, paper, a bag, a flipchart and a magic marker.

THE ACTIVITY

Put all the slips of paper into a bag. Invite each group member to draw one out and to complete the statement in writing. Explain that the statement must relate to the time spent together. When everyone has done this, collect all the pieces of paper and put them back in the bag again. Once again, invite each person to take a piece of paper from the bag. This time, ask a volunteer to read out what is written on their paper. Continue in this fashion until all the statements have been read out.

VARIATION

Prepare the beginning of five statements. Write the first one up on the flipchart. Invite each person in the group to complete the statement aloud. Write the beginning of a second statement up on the flipchart. Follow the same procedure until all five statements have been completed by everyone.

COMMENT

Compose the statements to draw out any information you want from the group. The activity can be made easier by reducing the number of statements to be completed.

USE ALSO FOR

Motivation and assessment and evaluation.

Shared learning

PREPARATION *materials needed*

Provide a soft ball or cushion for participants to throw to each other; you will also need a flipchart and a magic marker.

THE ACTIVITY

Form the group members into a circle. Explain that when someone has the ball he states something that he has learned, achieved or enjoyed during the session. Throw the ball to someone and he makes his statement. He then throws the ball to someone else. This continues until everyone has made a previously set number of statements.

Make a note on the flipchart of statements made and summarise them once they are all completed.

VARIATION

Divide the group into pairs. The pairs share what they have learned so far. After two or three minutes the pairs split, and each participant moves on to another partner and does the same again. Repeat this procedure a several times.

COMMENT

As a novelty when doing the variation, play soft music. When the music stops everyone changes partners. This is a another good way to reinforce learning by repetition.

USE ALSO FOR

Stimulating learning, motivation and assessment and evaluation.

AIMS

↑ To bring the session or session to an end
↑ To reinforce learning
↑ To find out what has been learned
↑ To reflect on what has been learned or achieved

10 What I like about ...

AIMS

⬆ To close the session or sessions

⬆ To end the group with positive feelings

⬆ To build self-esteem

PREPARATION *materials needed*

None.

THE ACTIVITY

Bring everyone into a circle. Ask each participant to consider the person on his right and think of something that he likes or admires about him. After allowing a moment for thought, start the process by making a statement about the person on your right, beginning with the words, 'What I like about ...'. An example might be, 'What I like about Hussain is his thoughtfulness.' That person now turns to the participant on his right and makes a statement about him in the same manner. This continues round the group.

VARIATION

Instead of focusing on individuals, have everyone make a statement about the group, beginning with the words: 'What I like about the group is ...'.

Alternatively, you could have one round of statements about individuals and a second round of statements about the group.

COMMENT

Some participants might feel slight embarrassment at praising others or being praised, and may need a little encouragement. However, this activity always ensures that the session ends on a positive and uplifting note.

USE ALSO FOR

Building trust, energising and motivation.

References and further reading

Adams S, 1989, *A Guide to Creative Tutoring*, Kogan Page Ltd, London

Bond T, 1986, *Games for Social and Life Skills*, reprinted 1990, Stanley Thornes, Cheltenham

Brandes D & Phillips H, 1979, *Gamesters' Handbook, 140 Games for Teachers and Group Leaders*, Hutchinson, London

Brandes D, 1983, *Gamesters' Handbook 2*, Hutchinson, London

Brandes D & Norris J, 1998, *Gamesters' Handbook 3*, Nelson Thornes, Cheltenham

Dynes R, 1990, *Creative Games in Groupwork*, Speechmark, Bicester

Hazouri SP & McLaughlin MS, 1993, *Warm Ups and Wind Downs*, Educational Media Corporation, Minneapolis

Kroehnert G, 1991, *100 Training Games*, McGraw-Hill, Sidney

Lynn, AB, 2002, *The Emotional Intelligence Activity Book*, AMACOM, New York

Moore AC, 1992, *The Game Finder*, Venture Publishing, State College PA

Pickles T, 1995, *Toolkit for Trainers*, Pavilion Publishing (Brighton), Brighton

West E, 1997, *201 Icebreakers*, McGraw Hill, New York